**The Ca
Wild R**

'We've been in scary situations before,' said Jake,
'but this feels so different. It's like falling into a
science fiction story. One moment you're with
friends in a normal situation; the next minute your
friends abandon you to survive in the wilderness . . .'

Jody and Jake's exciting trip down the Colorado
River has taken a frightening turn. Is it a joke, or is
someone trying to get rid of them?

The fourth Jody and Jake Mystery

The Case of the Wild River Ride

A Jody and Jake Mystery

Elizabeth Levy

KNIGHT BOOKS
Hodder and Stoughton

First published in the United States of America in 1981 by
Pocket Books, a Simon & Schuster division of
Gulf & Western Corporation, New York

First published in Great Britain by Knight Books 1983

British Library C.I.P.

Levy, Elizabeth
    The case of the wild river ride
    I. Title
    813′.54[J]   PZ7
    ISBN 0-340-32793-6

Printed and bound in Great Britain for Hodder and Stoughton Paper-
backs, a division of Hodder and Stoughton Ltd, Mill Road, Dunton
Green, Sevenoaks, Kent (Editorial Office: 47 Bedford Square, London,
WC1 3DP) by Cox and Wyman Ltd, Reading. Photoset by Rowland
Phototypesetting Ltd, Bury St Edmunds, Suffolk.

CONTENTS

1

MEET THE RIVER RATS

Harpo whimpered. He lay on the floor with his head on his paws, looking up at Jody. Groucho and Chico, the two cats, were cowering under the bed.

'They know we're leaving,' said Jake. 'As soon as we take out our knapsacks and sleeping bags they sense something is up.'

Jody bent down and patted Harpo on the head. Harpo, an odd cross between a poodle and a spaniel, wagged his tail slowly. 'Sorry, old boy, but no dogs allowed on a raft.'

'Maybe he can get on the plane instead of me,' said Jake. 'Exactly how little is this little plane we have to take?'

'Very,' said Jody. 'Eric said we take one of those tiny private planes.'

Jake turned a slightly odd colour of green. 'Whose idea was this anyhow?' he asked.

'Yours,' said Jody. 'You're the one who's always said you wanted to go down the Colorado River on a raft.'

'Oh, yeah. I sort of always thought we'd take a donkey or something to get to the river.'

'Cheer up,' said Jody. 'Maybe you'll love it.'

'I doubt it,' said Jake.

Just then Mrs Markson came into the room. 'Are you two finished packing?' she asked. 'We should leave for the airport soon.' She looked down. 'Why is Harpo cowering?'

'He's acting out what I'm feeling,' said Jake.

'Nervous about your adventure?' asked Mrs Markson. 'I know I would be. You're going down some of the biggest rapids in the world.'

'The rapids don't bother me,' said Jake. 'I'm more nervous about that stupid tiny plane.'

'There's no reason to call the plane stupid just because you're scared of it,' said Jody.

Mrs Markson smiled at her son. 'You'll be fine,' she said.

At the airport Mrs Markson gave both her children a final kiss. 'Have fun,' she said. 'I wish I could go with you. If I didn't have this stupid trial coming up, I'd take off with you.'

'Don't call your trial stupid just because it's long,' said Jake.

Mrs Markson ruffled Jake's curly red hair. 'And you – keep out of trouble.'

'Me!' protested Jake. 'It's Jody who usually finds trouble – even when we're on vacation.'

'Both of you, do whatever Eric asks,' said Mrs Markson. 'It was terrific of him to invite you, so don't give him any trouble.'

Eric Markson was Jody and Jake's cousin. Eric was a sophomore in college and loved the outdoors. He hoped to become a geologist. During the summers, he worked as a 'river rat', one of the guides who take tourists down the Colorado.

At Salt Lake City Jody and Jake got off their huge 747. Eric met them at their plane.

'I want to introduce you to your pilot,' he said after giving Jody a kiss on the cheek and shaking Jake's hand.

8

Jody and Jake looked around. No one was standing near-by. Eric ran a hand through his straight brown hair.

'Ah . . . where is he?' asked Jake timidly.

'Or she?' added Jody.

'You're looking at him,' said Eric. 'I just got my pilot's licence and I'm taking my boss's plane down to Moab for him.'

Jake groaned. 'You *just* got your pilot's licence?'

'Yeah. It came through last week. But you'll be perfectly safe.'

'I should have sent Harpo,' muttered Jake.

Eric looked at him strangely.

'Will we be your only passengers?' asked Jody.

'No,' said Eric. 'Two of the other guides are going to fly down with us. They'll meet us at the plane.'

They walked to the far end of the terminal, carrying their heavy backpacks with the sleeping bags tied on.

'Wait a minute,' said Jody, stopping by a green metal automatic newspaper dispenser. 'I want to get a Salt Lake City newspaper.'

'Why?' asked Eric. 'The whole point of this trip is to forget about civilisation.'

'But it'll be my last newspaper for five days,' said Jody. 'And besides, whenever I'm on a trip I like to get a local paper. It's like a souvenir.'

'It's something our dad does whenever he takes a trip,' said Jake. 'When he used to go to professional meetings he would always bring Jody back a paper. I always got a T-shirt.'

'Come on,' said Jody. 'Dad brought us presents too. He still does.'

Jody and Jake's parents were divorced. Their father was a psychologist in New York and Jody and Jake spent several weeks every summer and Christmas vacations with him.

Jody put a quarter in the machine and took out the paper. She slipped it next to the metal frame of her backpack and then hoisted her backpack onto her shoulders. Eric led the way through the terminal and out across the wide parking lot.

'Are we walking to Moab?' asked Jake. He had to shout to be heard over the loud noise of the airplanes taking off and landing.

'No. The private airfield is just over there,' said Eric. 'You can see our plane. It's the one with the blue and yellow stripes.'

'That's a plane?' said Jake.

'It does look a little small,' said Jody, sounding doubtful for the first time. From that distance the tiny Cessna Station-air looked as if it could easily fit into one of the passenger seats of the 747.

'Isn't she a beauty?' said Eric proudly.

'Why "she"?' asked Jody.

Eric shrugged his shoulders. 'I guess it's a holdover from when men used to call their boats "she".'

Eric checked the engine. Jake put down his backpack and rested on it. Jody stood beside him. Even close up, the plane still looked very small. Suddenly they heard a voice shout.

'Hey, Eric, who invented the first airplane that didn't fly?'

'The Wrong Brothers,' said Jake without even looking around.

'I knew you two would get along,' said Eric. 'Jody and Jake, meet Alison Hope, my fellow river rat.'

'I didn't know women were river guides,' said Jake. 'Whoops – my mom and Jody will kill me for saying that.'

'That's okay,' said Alison. 'There never used to be, but now there're quite a few of us.'

'Actually,' said Eric, 'Alison is one of the best there is. She grew up in the canyons.'

'Where's Jesse?' asked Alison.

'Jesse is the other guide,' Eric explained to Jake and Jody. 'He's always late.'

'He was talking about getting a helicopter to fly him to the glacier field near Sundance,' said Alison. 'It's illegal because of the avalanche danger, but Jesse *would* try it.'

'Jesse's got a lot more courage than sense,' said Eric.

'I wouldn't call being a daredevil courage,' said Alison sharply.

'That sounds like something Jody would say,' said Jake.

Jody and Alison smiled at each other. Alison was a tall woman with long auburn hair and a wide, open face with freckles and high cheekbones. She looked as though she could be immediately transported back to frontier America and fit right in.

'There's Jesse!' said Eric, pointing to someone loping toward the plane. He seemed to be sprouting loose clothes. His sleeping bag was unravelling as he ran, and his backpack hung perilously off one shoulder.

'Hi, gang!' he shouted as he got closer. 'Sorry I'm late. Now, Alison, don't give me that dirty look. That's no way to start the season.'

Alison smiled as if she couldn't help herself. Jesse was one of the most beautiful men Jody had ever seen outside the movies. He had straight blond hair streaked by the sun and bright blue eyes the colour of the sky on a perfect fall day.

'You must be Jody,' said Jesse. 'You're our guinea pigs.'

'That's the way to gain their confidence,' said Alison, sarcastically.

'Well, they are,' said Jesse.

'We know,' said Jody.

Jody and Jake had been invited on the river trip before the official tourist season started. Eric, Jesse, and Alison wanted to make one practice trip, and Eric had talked the others into taking two non-paying customers as passengers so they could get the feel of taking care of actual paying guests.

'Come on,' said Eric. 'Let's get this show on the road. Jake, why don't you take the seat next to me?'

Jake climbed the stairs into the plane. 'Well, as the condemned said when he approached the electric chair, "This is it." Get it, "sit".'

Alison laughed.

Jody groaned. 'Between Alison and Jake on this trip we're going to get our fill of puns.'

'Never throw a pun at a friend,' said Alison. 'It might be loaded.'

They all climbed into the tiny plane and took their seats. The seats were so close that Jody's knees were touching Jesse's. He smiled at her.

'As Bette Davis once said,' said Jesse, '"Fasten your seatbelts. It's gonna be a bumpy ride."'

2

WHAT'S GREEN AND DANGEROUS?

Jake's knuckles turned white as he gripped the edge of the seat. There were no armrests as there would be on a big commercial jet. There was so little insulation in the plane that the engine sounded as if it were inside Jake's head.

They taxied out to the runway. In the distance Jake could see the big commercial jets and he felt as if he had hitched a ride with a pigmy.

'Are you okay?' asked Eric.

Jake swallowed hard. 'Sure,' he said, but his voice ended up in a high squeak as the plane took off. Jake looked out. From his seat next to Eric it was like sitting in the front seat of a car. The view spread out underneath him with a 180-degree perspective. He could see the Great Salt Lake beneath him and the Mormon Tabernacle.

Eric put the plane into a steady incline as they rose to climb the high mountains that surround Salt Lake.

'Hey, look at that snow!' said Jake.

'That's where I was skiing yesterday,' said Jesse. 'Jody, if you look closely you might see my ski tracks.'

Jody didn't answer. She was looking out the window. Her

lips were tight and she seemed to be trying to see beyond the mountains.

Jake half-turned in his seat. 'Jody, guess what? I don't feel scared at all. I guess it was just one of those things that was more scary to think about than to do.'

'Great,' said Jody tersely.

'How long will it take us to get to Moab?' Jake asked.

'Just half an hour,' said Eric. 'But it would take five hours to drive over the mountains and around Soldier Summit. That's why so many Westerners fly these days.'

'Just half an hour,' said Jake. 'I wish it were longer.' Jake looked out the window again. They were now flying at about 12,000 feet. The towns and buildings were fewer and farther apart, with long stretches of dry-looking red clay in between.

'What's that?' asked Jake, pointing to a large building complex in the middle of nowhere.

'That's the Utah State Prison in Provo,' said Jesse. 'When they lock you up . . . That's where Gary Gilmore was shot.'

'Do you see that, Jody?' asked Jake. 'It's a historic sight.'

'No,' said Jody.

Jake turned around again in his seat. Jody seemed to be having trouble swallowing.

'You mean no, it's not a historic sight or no, you didn't see it?' asked Jake.

'I don't know what I meant,' said Jody, sounding miserable. 'I just want to get out of this airplane. I'm scared out of my wits.'

Jake giggled. 'I'm sorry,' he said.

'It's not nice to laugh at her,' said Jesse. 'Lots of people get scared in small planes.'

'I'm not usually like this,' said Jody.

'You can say that again,' said Jake.

'Try not to look directly down,' said Alison. 'Look across at the horizon.'

14

'I'm trying,' said Jody as she stared straight ahead.

Every once in a while out of the plane window a streak of green showed.

'That's the river,' said Eric. 'The Green River off to the left. We'll put in farther down.'

'Do you see it, Jody?' asked Jake.

'Yes,' said Jody. She sounded very frightened.

'This isn't like my sister,' said Jake. 'She's usually not scared of *anything*.'

'Eric's told us about her,' said Alison. 'He said you've got quite a reputation for solving mysteries.'

'Their mom is a top criminal lawyer,' said Eric.

'Is that so?' said Jesse. 'I don't remember anyone telling me anything about that. Do you ever get involved in her cases?'

'Does *she* ever,' said Jake.

'Really?' said Jesse. 'Tell me about it.'

'Not right now,' said Jody in a choked voice.

'Are you going to be sick?' asked Jesse worriedly. He was sitting the closest to Jody.

'I hope not,' said Jody through gritted teeth. Jesse got out a plastic-lined paper bag and handed it to her.

'Here. Just in case,' he said.

Jody looked at him gratefully. Then, seconds later, she threw up, neatly managing to get it all in the bag.

'Bull's-eye!' said Jesse. 'That was close timing.'

Jody felt both embarrassed and nauseated. It was a terrible combination.

Jesse took out his canteen and handed it to Jody. 'The best river rats always come prepared. Take a sip of water. It'll make you feel better.'

'Are you all right?' Jake asked anxiously. 'I'm sorry I teased you.'

'I'm fine,' said Jody.

'Don't be embarrassed,' said Alison. She smiled at Jody warmly.

Jody took a sip out of Jesse's canteen. The cool water tasted good.

'We're coming in for a landing,' said Eric. 'Everybody fasten your seatbelt.'

'Mine was never unfastened,' said Jody, beginning to feel better. She looked down. 'Where's the airport?'

'Uh, you see that Nissen hut?' asked Eric.

'Oh, no,' said Jody, looking down at a dirt field with two broken lines. 'That's not what what we're landing on, is it?' she asked, nearly pleading.

'Just close your eyes and we'll be down,' said Eric.

Jody's face looked horrified. Jesse gave Jody his hand to hold. Jody held on to it so tight her fingernails left an impression in Jesse's palm.

Finally Eric brought the plane to a rather bouncing stop. Jesse reached across with his free hand and tapped Jody's shoulder lightly. 'You can open your eyes now,' he said.

Jody slowly opened her eyes. Jake turned around and smiled at his sister. 'Remember, you were the one who told me I might love the plane trip, and I did.'

'Don't remind me,' said Jody.

'Don't be upset,' said Alison. 'A lot of people are afraid in small planes. It makes you feel out of control.'

'That's one feeling Jody never likes,' said Jake. Then he looked at his sister a little more sympathetically. 'You do still look a little green,' he said. 'Are you sure you're all right?'

'Yes,' said Jody shortly. 'I'm fine. Everybody stop worrying about me.'

Jake turned to Alison. 'We'd better leave her alone. Do you know what's green and dangerous?'

'No,' answered Alison. 'What?'

'A thundering herd of pickles,' said Jake.

'This is going to be some raft trip,' said Eric. 'Just what we needed – two jokers in the pack and one daredevil.'

3

JAKE DOES
SOMETHING STUPID

High in the mountains when the snow starts to melt it trickles downhill. In the beginning nothing looks like a river. Then the trickles find each other and they keep finding the easiest way downhill.

Without the use of motors, Jake and Jody were about to take that downhill ride in a ten-foot rubber raft. Their journey was to start on the Green River and take them to where the Green met the mighty Colorado. Where the two mighty rivers met, they turned into an incredible force that roared through the Grand Canyon.

The two rafts were tied up just below a bridge on the Green River. There was so much equipment to be loaded for their two-week trip, it didn't look possible that everything would ever get into the rafts.

Eric stood frowning at the piles in front of him.

'Can I help?' Jody asked.

'Thanks,' said Eric. 'Jesse was supposed to help me with the checklist, but I don't know where he is. He and Jake seem to have disappeared.'

'What about Alison?' asked Jody.

'She had something she needed to do in town,' said Eric. 'Some last-minute phone call. She'll meet us. She's dependable. Alison always tells you exactly what she's going to do.'

Jody smiled. She wondered if her cousin Eric and Alison had a romance going or if one would develop on the trip. 'Have you worked with Alison before?' Jody asked.

Eric shook his head. 'No. She's never worked for an outfitter before, but I've seen her run rapids in a kayak. She's one of the best – but she's not out to prove anything. She doesn't do it just for the danger.'

'I take it that's your opinion of Jesse,' said Jody. 'You and Alison don't seem to like him.'

Eric didn't answer. He looked down at the list he held in his hand. 'How about giving me some help with my check-list?'

'Okay,' said Jody, recognising a change of subject when she saw it.

Jody went to each item and shouted it out to Eric: 'Three cooking pots, two frying pans, one long-handled wooden spoon, one reflector oven and baking pan.' She went through all the cooking equipment and moved on to the next pile. 'Two first-aid kits,' she said. 'Do you want me to open them?'

'No,' said Eric. 'I checked them last night. They're complete – snakebite kit, suction cups, antibiotics – the works.'

'What do we do if we have an accident?' asked Jody.

'That's one of the reasons we take two boats,' said Eric. 'If one's damaged, we can get out in the other – or go for help. I've taken a pretty rigorous first-aid course. In fact, so have Alison and Jesse. We're prepared.'

'That's the Boy Scout motto,' Jody said. 'If I remember, you were a Scout.'

'I was,' said Eric.

Just then they heard a shout from under the bridge. *'Off we go into the wild blue yonder!'* sang out a voice.

Jesse came floating down the river in an inner tube. He waved to Jody and Eric and started to paddle his way to the shore. Jake came paddling behind. At this point the river was a slow-moving greenish grey, but the current was still powerful.

Jesse came to shore easily and turned to see where Jake was. Jake was paddling with his hands furiously, but he didn't seem to be making much progress toward the shoreline.

'Jake, come in!' shouted Jody. She turned to Eric. 'He shouldn't be out in the middle of the river, should he?' she asked.

'No,' said Eric sharply. 'Jesse, you stupid . . .'

'Hey, we just went in for a couple of hundred feet – and the river's so calm here, no one can get in trouble.'

'Oh, yeah?' said Eric. 'Then how come he's stuck in the middle of the river?'

'I'm not making much progress,' admitted Jake, shouting from the inner tube. His legs were sticking out of the side with only his bottom in the river.

'Hold on,' said Eric.

'I am,' said Jake, holding on to the side of the inner tube desperately. His paddling made his balance lopsided and he almost ended up face down in the river. 'Whoops!' cried Jake, as the tube started to roll over. 'This is not a very steady ship.'

'Jake, don't do anything stupid,' warned Jody from the shore.

'I'm afraid it's too late for that,' shouted Jake.

Jody started to run down the side of the river. Jake was being carried down the river at a fairly fast pace.

Eric ran to one of the piles of supplies and grabbed one of three long rescue ropes.

'Jake!' shouted Jesse. 'Don't panic. There are no rapids for miles. You have nothing to worry about.'

'Except tipping over and drowning,' muttered Eric.

'He can swim,' said Jesse. Then he looked over at Jody. 'He *can* swim, can't he?' he asked anxiously.

'Yes, of course,' said Jody, 'but . . .'

'Knowing how to swim and knowing how to fight a river current are two different things,' snapped Eric.

'*Excuse me!*' shouted Jake from the middle of the river. 'Could you three maybe stop arguing and tell me what I'm supposed to do? I can't seem to make this stupid inner tube come to shore.'

'I'm going to throw you a rope!' shouted Eric.

'That sounds like a very good idea,' said Jake.

Eric took the coiled rope and threw it with a strong underarm fling of his wrist. It came close to Jake's tube, but fell about a foot short.

'I can't reach it,' shouted Jake, drifting farther out into the middle of the river.

'Here. Let me try!' said Jesse as Eric hauled in the rope hand over hand.

'I suppose you *do* have a better arm,' said Eric, sounding as if he hated to give Jesse the benefit of the doubt.

He handed the now wet rope to Jesse. Jesse's impish face took on a serious expression as he judged the distance between himself and Jake and tried to add on how fast Jake was moving. Then he flung the rope out in a sidearm gesture. It landed just ahead of Jake, so that Jake had several seconds to prepare himself to grab the rope.

Jake held on to the rope as Jesse slowly hauled Jake and his inner tube to shore.

'Whew!' said Jake. 'That's a little more trouble than I thought.'

'It's Jesse's fault,' said Eric. 'He should never have taken you out in an inner tube.'

'Oh, come on, Eric,' said Jesse. 'Don't make a big deal out of it. I'm sorry. I just thought Jake and I would surprise you by arriving by inner tube.'

'Some surprise,' said Eric.

'I said I'm sorry,' repeated Jesse, looking embarrassed.

'Look, Eric, it was my fault as much as Jesse's,' said Jake. 'The river looked so calm, I never thought I'd have trouble getting to shore.'

'All right,' said Eric finally. 'We'll give both you and Jody river-swimming lessons as soon as we take off. Right now let's finish packing.'

Jesse smiled at Jody – his most charming smile. 'I'm really sorry I got your brother in trouble,' he said.

'Let's help Eric,' said Jody shortly. She didn't like people who took unnecessary chances.

4

JUST SALMON
YOUR STRENGTH

The two rafts were loaded and there was nothing to do but wait for Alison. Eric paced up and down the dock, fuming. Jody pulled out her newspaper.

Jesse sat down beside her. 'Can I see the funnies?' he asked.

'I don't know what page they're on,' said Jody shortly.

'You don't have to snap my head off,' said Jesse.

Jody looked into his blue eyes. She hadn't meant to speak sharply. She felt herself blushing. She didn't want Jesse to think she was a Little Miss Goody Two-Shoes. 'I wasn't snapping,' she said. 'I really don't know what page they are on. It's a Salt Lake City paper. I picked it up at the airport, but I forgot about it.'

'Here,' said Jesse, taking the newspaper from her. 'I'll find it.' Jesse took the paper and quickly folded it.

As he held the paper up, Jody, who would read the label on the toothpaste if she had nothing else to read, started to read the stories on the back page. 'Prison Breakout! Suspected Killer Loose.'

'Hey, I wonder if that was the prison we flew over,' asked Jody. 'Let me see the front page.'

'What?' asked Jesse. 'Wait a minute. Let me just finish "Doonesbury".'

'It's my paper,' protested Jody, but before Jesse could give it to her, Alison arrived. She glanced guiltily at them.

'Where's Eric?' she asked.

'He's pacing around here somewhere,' said Jesse.

Eric and Jake appeared from a path along the river.

'Eric, I'm really sorry,' said Alison, sounding almost desperate. 'I had trouble getting the jeep started.'

'You know,' said Jake, 'if you want a good car, you can't expect it to be jeep.'

Alison groaned. Then she looked at Jake. 'How come you look damp? Did you take a swim?'

'He took a little unscheduled ride on an inner tube,' said Jody.

'Yeah. I could have ended up in California,' admitted Jake.

Alison looked over at Jesse. 'I bet it was your idea,' she said.

'I've already been in trouble,' said Jesse, 'and I admitted I was wrong.' He handed Jody back her paper.

'Okay,' said Eric, 'let's not argue about that now. It's already eleven A.M. If we want to get to our first campsite, we should start off now.'

Eric went to the pile of life jackets and started to hand them out. 'We won't hit any rapids until tomorrow, but I want everyone to wear his or her life jacket all the time.'

'Yes, sir,' said Jesse. 'Come on, Eric, lighten up. You sound like you're a stewardess on an airplane. It's just us.'

'Look, Jesse, the whole point of the trip is to get us ready for the tourists. We'll be making this trip about a dozen times this summer, and this is our chance to iron out all the kinks. I want to run it exactly the way we would if Jody and Jake were paying.'

'Okay, okay – my mistake. Again,' said Jesse. 'I'm sorry. It just seemed a little silly to wear the life jackets today.'

'Eric's right,' said Alison. 'We should treat this like a trip during the regular season. After all, we'll never know how many clinkers we have on a trip . . .'

'Clinkers?' asked Jody. 'What's a clinker?'

'A clinker is when we have someone who makes the trip miserable for everyone else – either a complainer or a real dummy – someone who is always falling overboard and getting into trouble,' explained Alison.

'A dummy is a crummy,' said Jake.

'Exactly,' said Eric. 'Let's get going.'

'Jody, you go in Jesse's boat. I think we'll keep Jesse and Jake separate for a while. Jake, you can go with me and Alison. We can switch the order each day. Each of us will carry a whistle. Three short toots means we want to get together for a confab. One long toot means you're in trouble.'

Jody put on her bright orange life jacket. It was much thicker in front than in back, and it made her feel as if she looked like a stuffed koala bear.

'Why are they so thick?' she asked as she struggled to close the snaps.

'To make sure that you float face up, not face down,' said Jesse. 'We spent a lot of money on them to get the best. It's worth it. These will keep you floating face up until you can get to shore – or for hours if need be. They're nylon so they won't get waterlogged, and they're made of the best foam.'

'That gives me confidence,' said Jody.

'With luck you won't need them,' said Jesse, 'but when we go through Big Drop in Cataract Canyon, anything can happen.'

'I'll remember to wear it then,' said Jody.

'Eric's right,' said Jesse. 'It's not a bad idea to get in the habit of wearing them all the time. For a change I shot my mouth off before thinking.'

Jody got into the front of the raft. She perched on the side and found it hot on her thighs. 'Ouch!' she cried.

'Whoops,' said Jesse. 'I should have warned you to put a towel under there. These rafts heat up very quickly. Did you put on suntan lotion?'

'No,' said Jody. 'but I don't burn. I tan easily. It's Jake who's got the red hair. He's got all our suntan lotion.'

Jesse handed her a plastic bottle. 'Put this on,' he insisted.

Jody picked up the bottle. It was a sunscreen labelled 'Maximum Protection'. 'I don't need this,' she said. 'I want to get a tan.'

'Don't argue,' said Jesse. 'The sun is wicked. Remember, we're going through desert country. You'll be getting wet and may think you're not burning, but you will be.'

Jody looked at him doubtfully. Jesse had a deep copper-coloured tan. 'Believe me,' said Jesse, 'we're going to be on the river several days. You'll get plenty of sun.'

'Okay,' said Jody, secretly amused that Jesse took a suntan so seriously while he seemed to take nothing else seriously. She spread the lotion on evenly.

Once they were drifting out on the river Jody had to admit that the sun was hot. She kept dipping her headscarf in the water and retying the cool wet cloth around her neck.

Jesse rowed smoothly, bracing his legs so that he could use the power in the lower half of his body as well as his arms. The current in the river helped move them along, but to Jody, who had expected a wild river ride, this slow-moving, greenish grey, dirty water was a disappointment.

'I'll tell you what,' said Jesse, 'why don't you take a swim?'

Jody looked at him doubtfully. 'I don't want to end up like Jake, floating halfway to California.'

'No, I'm serious,' said Jesse. 'You should take a dip with your life jacket on, so that you get used to it – and it'll cool you off.'

'Are you sure you're not just trying to get me in trouble so Jake and I will be equal?' asked Jody.

Jesse didn't answer. Instead, he blew on his whistle three sharp toots. The second raft was only a few hundred feet ahead. Eric backrowed his raft in place while Jody and Jesse caught up.

'Don't you think we should give Jody and Jake a chance for a river swim?'

'Is it dangerous to swim on a full stomach?' asked Jake, munching a cookie.

'It's better to swim in the water. Anyhow, we haven't had lunch yet,' said Alison, taking the cookie from him.

'Actually, Jesse's right,' said Eric. 'The best way to learn about swimming in the river is to do it. Then you won't panic if we happen to have an accident. Why don't you both go overboard. Take a line with you so you won't have trouble getting back into the boat.'

'I've already had my share of that in the inner tube,' said Jake.

'It's much safer with a life jacket on,' said Eric.

'All right,' said Jake, 'if you say so.' Jake held his nose and rolled off the side of the raft into the water. His life jacket made him immediately pop up and held his neck way above the water line.

'Come on in, Jody, the water's freezing,' he said.

'That's because it's still freshly melted snow at this time of year,' explained Jesse. 'Go on, Jody. It's fun.'

Jody jumped off the raft and into the muddy water. Without even moving a muscle to swim, she began to float at about five miles an hour downstream. The life jacket held her upright.

'This is neat!' cried Jody. 'It feels a little like walking on the moon.'

'Hey, Jake!' shouted Alison. 'What did the moon say to the star?'

'Boy, are you far out!' answered Jake. 'Jody is right. I feel like an astronaut. It feels more like walking than swimming.' Jake's legs were directly underneath him and he felt as if he were bounding up and down the river.

'Alison!' he shouted. 'Which is heavier, a half moon or a full moon?'

'A half moon,' answered Alison, 'because it's lighter under a full moon.'

Jody groaned. 'I'm glad you two are in the same boat.' Jody floated on her back and let her toes wiggle in front of her. Jesse looked down at her from the raft. They floated along at the same speed.

'You look very happy in there,' he said.

'It is an absolutely terrific sensation,' said Jody.

'Well, it can be a little less terrific when there are rocks in the way and you're going through rapids, but the main thing to remember is not to panic. The river will carry you out of trouble. And always remember that somewhere up ahead there's a calm spot just like now. If you get thrown out of the raft, face downstream and go into your astronaut position. It's a good trick to tell yourself that it's just like walking on the moon. Then you'll remember to keep your feet beneath you. That way your feet, not your backbone, will bounce off the rocks. The main thing is to learn that you can't fight powerful currents, so don't try. Conserve your strength and try to avoid crashing into rocks until you get to quieter water.'

'You take this pretty seriously, Jesse,' said Jody.

'Well, I don't want to see you get hurt,' said Jesse.

Jody glanced ahead at Eric and Alison in the raft ahead of

them. 'I wish you'd let Eric see that you're not just a daredevil,' she said.

'Oh, don't worry about my reputation,' laughed Jesse. 'Anyhow, I think you'd better come back into the boat now.'

'Why?' asked Jody. 'I could just float down the river the whole way.'

'Not and survive, you couldn't,' said Jesse. 'That water's cold. Hypothermia can sneak up on you.'

'Hypothermia? What's that?' asked Jody.

'The body loses its ability to regulate its temperature,' explained Jesse. 'It can happen much faster than you think. First you lose your coordination and your mind starts to go fuzzy. It can result in death.'

'Okay,' said Jody, 'you convinced me. I'm coming out. Jake!' she shouted. 'Jesse says we should get out.'

'He's right,' said Eric. 'You've had enough. Come back to the boat.'

Jake had got ahead of his raft. He tried to swim upstream, but made little headway.

'Don't try to go upstream,' shouted Alison. 'We'll get to you. Just salmon your strength.'

'I'd groan, but it's too much work,' said Jody as Jesse pulled her into the raft.

29

5

IT'S NOT MY BAG

They made camp around four o'clock. By that time Jody and Jake had got used to the sudden changes of riding a river through the canyons. They had learned that because the sun had only the slot of the canyon to shine down on them, they could be baking in almost intolerable heat at one moment and then shivering in gloomy wet shadows the next.

Jody was already grateful for Jesse's insistence on suntan lotion. Because of the reflection from the water and the canyon walls the sun burned odd parts – under the chin, even between the fingertips. Then, when the sun disappeared over the canyon rim, the temperature in the canyon bottom dropped twenty and thirty degrees. In a matter of minutes they were reduced from sweating to shivering.

Finding a campsite on the river was not the easiest of tasks. There were only a few places in the canyon where the river had carved out a wide enough space. Eric directed them to a stream bed where a little creek emerged between low cliffs two hundred yards back from the river. Back away from the stream bed were several patches of sand, where they could stretch out their sleeping bags. A grove of straight young cottonwood trees grew by the little creek, leaving a place to find firewood.

Jody helped Jesse bring the raft up out of the water. Jesse tied it carefully to a tree. 'We don't want to lose it if California suddenly decides it wants more electricity,' he said.

'What?' exclaimed Jody.

'Yeah. Our water level is decided by how much they decide to let out of Lake Powell and through the Glen Canyon dam. In fact, Eric has the computer readout with him. We'll study them tomorrow when we figure out our route through the rapids.'

'Computerised!' exclaimed Jody. 'And it looks so wild.'

'Oh, it's still wild,' said Alison. 'Wait till we hit our first rapids tomorrow.'

Jody unrolled her sleeping bag and went to get her sweat shirt out of her backpack. She pulled out the newspaper. It was crumpled.

'What's that?' asked Alison.

'It's my Salt Lake City newspaper,' said Jody. She explained about her habit of collecting local newspapers.

'A raft trip is no place for a newspaper,' said Alison. 'You're supposed to get away from civilisation.'

'That's what Eric told me,' said Jody.

'Well, he and I agree on a lot of things,' said Alison.

Jody again wondered whether Alison and Eric were going out together, but somehow Alison sounded distracted and almost distant. Jody wondered if maybe Eric and Alison had had a fight over Alison's being so late. Jody knew that fights could start over something small and escalate.

'Come on, Jody,' said Alison, 'let's set up the ladies' room. Unfortunately, for all of women's liberation, we still observe the old "ladies upstream, men downstream". You can help me shovel out our latrine.'

'Now doesn't that sound like fun?' said Jesse sarcastically.

'Meanwhile, you guys can start gathering the firewood. It's your turn to cook tonight,' said Alison.

She led Jody away through the cottonwoods. 'We don't want to get too far away,' warned Alison. 'Modesty doesn't go with mosquitoes. I hope you brought insect repellent.'

'It was on Eric's list,' said Jody.

'Trust Eric to be thorough,' said Alison. 'He's a good guide.'

'He says that you are a terrific person to run the rapids.'

'Yeah,' said Alison sarcastically. 'I can get through the tough parts with no problem. I have more of a problem when it's calm.'

'I know what you mean,' said Jody. 'Jake is always teasing me that I look for trouble, just because I'm good under pressure.'

'So Eric was telling me,' said Alison, shovelling. 'He says you've led a pretty exciting life for somebody so young.'

'I'm not so young,' objected Jody. 'How old are you?'

'Eighteen,' answered Alison. 'How old are you and Jake?'

'I'm fifteen and Jake's fourteen. Do you have any brothers or sisters?' Jody asked.

It seemed an innocent question, but Alison's usually open face suddenly looked guarded.

'Yeah, I have a brother,' said Alison.

'Are you close?' asked Jody.

'Not really,' said Alison. 'We're not alike at all.'

'Oh,' said Jody. Something about Alison's manner made her realise that Alison didn't particularly want to talk about her brother.

'Not everybody is as close as you and Jake,' said Alison. She sounded almost wistful.

'We get on each other's nerves too,' said Jody, wanting to sound sympathetic.

'Yeah, but you trust each other. That's the important thing.'

'I guess you're right,' said Jody. She had never examined her trust for Jake.

Alison handed the shovel to Jody. 'Your turn,' she said.

They finished building their latrine and came back out to join the guys, who already had a fire going.

The sunset seen from the river level was awesome. Shadows flowed into the canyon bottom as if Dracula's cape had been drawn over the sun. It was as if the sun had suddenly decided to desert them altogether, and it left nothing but a dark purple sky overhead – and the cold.

Jody got her down vest out of her backpack and put it on. 'It gets cold fast,' she said, shivering.

'My chilli will warm you up,' said Jesse, stirring his pot with a long-pronged fork. Some biscuits were baking in the reflector oven. Eric and Alison sat off to the side, talking quietly. Every once in a while Alison would look into the fire with that same troubled look that Jody had noticed earlier.

'Where's Jake?' asked Jody, looking around the campsite.

'Here I am,' said Jake. 'I was just seeing how far I could climb up, but then it got dark.'

'Actually, you shouldn't go off by yourself,' warned Jesse. 'We've got plenty of rattles and scorpions around, not to mention falling rocks.'

'I was just looking around,' said Jake defensively.

'Don't pick on him,' said Alison, coming out of her conversation with Eric. 'It's okay to explore.'

'Actually, if you climbed to the top, you'd find the Box Canyon where Butch Cassidy and the Sundance Kid used to hide out,' said Eric. 'Sometimes we take tours up there.'

'How do they get there?' asked Jake. 'I tried to climb up, but you would need expert climbing gear to get up those walls.'

'There's a hidden path about a quarter of a mile from here,' said Eric.

'It sounds fun,' said Jody. 'Can we climb it tomorrow morning?'

'*No!*' said Alison and Eric at the same time. They looked embarrassed to be agreeing with each other. Then they smiled.

'We'd lose a whole morning if you took a climb, and I'm anxious to get to our first rapids,' said Alison.

'Me too,' said Eric.

'I can't argue with that,' said Jesse. 'Come on. Let's eat.' Jesse filled their metal cups with his chilli.

Jake took a bite. It was so hot his eyes immediately began to water. 'I don't know why they call this "chilli".'

'It's delicious,' said Jody. Jesse blushed, and Jody realised that he had been worried they wouldn't like it. Eric agreed, and Jesse dug into his own plate with relish.

'One thousand mosquitoes can't be wrong,' said Jesse, swatting away the bugs that had suddenly descended on them like vultures.

Eric threw a heavy log on the fire. 'This should help keep them away.'

Alison swatted the bugs around her head. They formed a halo around her hair.

'What we need here is a bugaboo,' said Jake.

'What's a bugaboo?' asked Eric.

Alison giggled.

'Oh, no,' said Eric, 'not another pun!'

Jake paid no attention to his groans. 'You sneak up behind mosquitoes and scare them to death. That's a buga-boo.'

Jody and Jesse groaned in unison. 'Enough, enough!'

Eric reached for the bug spray and sprayed himself. 'These are getting really terrible. Let's say we all go to bed.'

'Good idea,' said Alison, 'because the beds will not come to us.'

'Actually, since they're sleeping bags, they could go any-where,' said Jesse.

'Do you know what the kangaroo said when it wouldn't jump into the adult kangaroo's pouch?' asked Jody.

'*It's not my bag!*' shouted Alison and Jesse in unison.

'Oh, no,' said Eric, putting his hands over his ears, 'it's catching!'

'What do you often catch, but never see?' asked Jake?

'A breeze,' said Alison, doubling over in laughter. It was as if sitting by the fire with the stars overhead had inflated their sense of humour so that no one could say a word without someone else thinking of a joke. Jody was laughing so hard her stomach hurt. She felt as if she had never been happier.

6

THINGS THAT GO
BUMP IN THE NIGHT

Jody blew up her air mattress and unrolled her sleeping bag.
She took off her sneakers. Before they had set off to sleep Eric
had warned them about scorpions. Scorpions liked to hide in
what seemed to them warm holes, so they were often found in
shoes. Eric gave them each sealable plastic bags in which to
put their sneakers. Jesse teased Eric that he was being overly
cautious.

'I've been on the river for years and I've never found a
scorpion in my shoe,' argued Jesse.

'Never mind,' said Eric, handing him a plastic bag. 'Better
safe than sorry.'

'Where have I heard that before,' said Jesse, but he took
the bag.

Jody remembered Eric's advice and put her sneakers in the
bag. Then she crawled into her sleeping bag. The sound of
the river was comforting and Jody fell sound asleep within
seconds of lying down. She woke up when she heard something moving in the stand of cottonwood trees. Jody almost
always woke up alert. She immediately knew where she was.

She tried to locate the sound. She knew that the canyon caused strange echoes.

Jody had found a place to sleep a little bit away from the others. When she was camping she liked to feel that she was alone. She had a digital watch with a light built in. She pressed the light. 11:43 P.M. The fire was still smouldering. Eric had said that it would help to keep the mosquitoes away, but Jody could hear and feel them just above her head. She had gone to sleep with her T-shirt wrapped around her head and neck, but it had come undone in her sleep and she could feel two big bites on the back of her neck.

Then she heard the sound again that had awakened her – a crackling of twigs. Jesse had told her that some mountain elk sometimes manoeuvred down the canyon path to the river for water. There were no bears in the vicinity and only an occasional mountain lion. Jody's first thought was of scorpions. But only in science fiction would a scorpion be so big as to make that much noise.

Jody felt for her flashlight, which she had carefully put by her sleeping bag. Her hands curled around it. She found the switch. She beamed the light in the direction of the cotton-wood trees. She couldn't see anything. Then she turned sharply. There seemed to be a noise right near her sleeping bag. It sounded as if an animal might be burrowing in her pack. She heard a sharp crack as if a twig had broken. Suddenly something grazed her hand and her flashlight rolled out of reach.

Jody quickly brought her hand back into her sleeping bag. She wasn't sure what had touched her hand. Had it been human? Insect? She was scared to put her hand out of the bag for the flashlight. Finally, she regained her courage and searched around for the flashlight but couldn't find it.

Jody peered out of the sleeping bag, but the moon had disappeared from the narrow canyon and it was almost impossible to see more than a few feet in front of her. Jody thought about raking her hand along the stones next to her sleeping bag, but the thought of scorpions made her decide to pull her hand back inside.

Maybe it was nothing. Jody thought to herself. She snuggled back down in her sleeping bag, covered her head, and fell back asleep.

Jody woke up with the first light of dawn. She unwound herself from her improvised mosquito netting and sat up in her sleeping bag. Her flashlight was standing upright next to her. Jody stared at it. She didn't know how it got there.

She walked over to her pack. Her little pocket mirror lay on the ground. It had been stepped on and shattered. Jody picked it up. 'Oh, no! Seven years' bad luck!'

'What's the matter?' asked Jesse. He had been sleeping near her.

'Something or someone was in my pack and my mirror's broken.'

'What?' asked Jesse. He got out of his sleeping bag and went over to Jody. 'Anything else missing?'

Jody quickly rifled through her pack. 'My newspaper!' said Jody with a puzzled look on her face.

'Your newspaper!' said Jesse. 'A newspaper stolen. What evil lurks in the hearts . . .'

'It's not funny,' said Jody. 'Why would someone break my mirror and steal my newspaper?'

'What's going on?' asked Eric. 'Is something wrong?'

'The great newspaper caper,' said Jesse. 'Someone took Jody's newspaper.'

'Good riddance,' said Eric. 'Besides, I told you raft trips were no place to bring a newspaper.'

'Did you take it?' demanded Jody. 'Someone came near my pack last night, and when I took out my flashlight to look, it got knocked from my hand.'

'That doesn't sound much like a joke,' said Alison.

'It wasn't. And they broke my mirror,' said Jody, glad to have someone take her seriously.

'But you've got your flashlight in your hand now,' pointed out Eric. 'It didn't go very far.'

'I know,' said Jody, blushing. 'When I woke up it was right by my sleeping bag. It's very strange.'

'Come on,' complained Jake. 'Even you can't make a big mystery out of a stolen day-old newspaper. Forget it.'

'I'm not making a big mystery of it,' said Jody. She felt silly. She didn't want Eric, Alison, and Jesse to think that she was the kind of person who had to make a big melodrama out of the slightest thing that happened.

'Okay,' said Jody reluctantly, 'forget it.'

'Thatta girl,' said Alison, clapping her on the shoulder. 'Let's have some breakfast and get back on the river. I'm starving. I slept like a log. There's nothing like the sound of the river to put me out like a light.'

'I'm starving too,' said Jesse. 'Besides, I can't wait to get to our first rapids. We should hit Cataract Canyon this afternoon.'

'Right,' said Eric. 'The graveyard of the Colorado.'

7

A LIVE BODY IN THE COLORADO GRAVEYARD

They had stopped for lunch at a sandbar where the Colorado met the Green. The sun now had clouded over. A layer of damp clouds hung from the top of one cliff to the other like a dingy cloth. It started to drizzle. Jody's life jacket felt damp and cold.

The Colorado ran calm and straight for the next four miles. Then it made a sharp left turn and suddenly Jody could hear the noise.

'Do you hear it?' shouted Jesse.

It was a low, deep sound. 'Raging river' had always sounded to Jody like a cliché, but the cliché existed because it was true. The river sounded as if it were furious, angry to be held between the deep walls of the canyon.

They were now about fifty yards above the rapids. Jesse and Eric both dipped their hands in the water in order to get a better grip on the oar handles. Alison brought her raft up close. If Eric and Jesse misread the river and got into trouble, Alison would be able to correct their mistake and rescue them.

'Is there anything I'm supposed to do?' shouted Jody, trying to be heard over the sound of the rapid.

'Hold on,' said Eric. 'If we tip over, don't panic. Your life jacket will hold you up. Just float through the rapids in the position we showed you. These rapids end in a nice pool and Alison will be able to pick you up without much trouble.

Jody looked ahead. She could see the tail waves from the water as they hit rocks and bounced back. As the water twisted among the rocks, there was a glossy 'tongue'. Jody knew they would ride that tongue and then have to man-oeuvre through a series of smaller rocks.

Jesse pointed the raft so it hit the tongue smoothly. The front end of the raft swooped up into the air as the water carried it down. Jesse and Eric used their oars to keep the raft balanced and away from the rocks.

Jody felt as if time were standing still. It probably only took seconds to go through the rapids, but it couldn't be measured in time. Every foot had seemed to last several minutes.

When they hit the smooth pool she looked back and watched Alison straining at the oars as she and Jake bounced through the rapid. Jake had a huge grin on his face.

Jody looked ahead. Another rapid was facing them. It was choked with boat-sized rocks. Jesse pulled hard to the left, getting them ready to run through.

Suddenly Jody screamed.

She spotted something bright orange clinging to one of the rocks. 'Somebody's there!' she cried.

Eric moved up to the front of the raft. 'Jesse,' he shouted, 'there's somebody on the big rock to the left, right near the end. We'll have to pick him up.'

'How the——' Jesse started to say, but there wasn't any time to talk. He pulled hard to squeeze in among the rocks on the left where there was a clear entry. The man or woman –

Jody couldn't tell which – was clinging to the rock in the middle. Now going through the rapids no longer seemed fun, but a grim rescue.

'Get him from the upstream side,' shouted Eric.

Jesse's muscles strained as he tried to make the boat shift through the powerful water.

Eric took out the nylon rescue rope and held it coiled in his hand. They were now nearly on top of the person.

'Grab hold!' shouted Eric.

Jody just had time to see a pair of terrified eyes before they swept past the man. She looked back and saw that he had caught hold of the rope.

Jesse shot their raft down the middle and caught an eddy against a left bank beach. Eric and Jody reached down and helped the man into their raft. He was coughing and sputtering. His small day pack was wound around his arm. Above them, Jake and Alison were staring. The man had seemed to appear from nowhere.

'Get him fresh water,' said Eric.

Jody got her canteen and held it to the man's lips. He seemed to be a man in his early twenties. He had short blond hair. His hair was so streaked by the sun it looked as if it had been dyed. He took a sip of the water gratefully.

'I'm all right,' he croaked, but his lips were sunburned and he seemed to be in mild shock.

'We've got to get you out of your wet clothes,' said Eric.

Meanwhile, Alison and Jake had come through the rapids with no trouble. They landed their raft on the sandbar.

'What in the world!' demanded Alison. 'Where's his boat?'

'We just found the guy,' snapped Jesse.

'I'm okay. I'm okay,' muttered the man. 'Just give me a moment to catch my breath.'

'Come on,' said Eric gently. He helped the man out of the

42

raft and onto dry land. 'Get the first-aid kit and my sleeping bag,' he said.

Eric and Jesse got the man out of his wet clothes and wrapped him in Eric's sleeping bag. Alison and Jody gathered driftwood so they could make a fire and dry the man's clothes and help him warm up.

The man lay down and closed his eyes.

'I think he's in shock,' said Jesse.

'We'll have to let him rest before we can ask him questions,' said Eric.

Jake had stood to the side, strangely silent. Jody went up to him.

'Who do you think he is?' she asked.

'I don't know. What was he doing in the middle of the wilderness?' asked Jake. 'Trust you.'

'What does that mean?' asked Jody indignantly.

'I don't know. We were finally having just a normal fun vacation, and you manage to find a stranger who needs help in the middle of nowhere,' said Jake.

'I didn't find him,' objected Jody. 'He found us. He was just clinging to that rock for dear life.'

'It's weird, that's all. I was kidding this morning about your newspaper. But this is too much,' said Jake. He kicked at a loose rock with his foot. Then he caught Jody staring at the man lying on Eric's sleeping bag. Her face was full of concern.

'I'm sorry,' he said.

Jody looked at her brother in surprise. 'For what?' she asked.

'I was being selfish,' he said. 'I was just having so much fun I didn't want real life to butt in. But even I can see it's not your fault.'

'Thanks,' said Jody, 'but I know how you feel. It's as if it's an intrusion. We were in such a little world, but we couldn't

43

have left him stranded. And besides, maybe he'll be okay and we can just take him down the river with us.'

'Right,' said Jake. 'Besides, maybe he even knows a few good jokes.'

8

A SHOCKING STORY

Jody and Jake walked back over to the group. The man rose to a half-sitting position. He kept protesting that he was okay. Alison improvised a shade over him made up of ground sheets, and she took several life jackets and tucked them under his back for support.

'Where's the young lady who fished me out?' the stranger asked.

'It was Jody who spotted you first,' said Eric.

Jody came to the front. The man made an effort to get to his feet as if to shake her hand. Jody crouched down and took his hand.

'Where's your boat?' asked Jesse, looking downstream. 'We'll try to rescue it for you.'

'Do you have a gun?' the man asked.

Everyone stared at him.

'No,' said Eric finally, thinking the man was in shock. 'Why?'

The man barked a hoarse laugh.

'Look, are you sure you're feeling all right?' asked Alison in a worried voice. 'I think you're babbling.'

'I don't blame you for thinking that,' said the man. 'Wait

till the sergeant hears what happened. He won't believe it.'

'Sergeant?' asked Jody. She knew that there were some army bases nearby. In fact, they were near the spot where there once had been atomic testing and where several nuclear warheads were rumoured to be buried.

'Who are you?' Jody asked.

The man closed his eyes, as if the question were too much for him. Then he opened them again. He seemed to stare at Jody for several seconds, as if something about her helped him focus.

'My name's Matt Diamond. Believe it or not, I'm a sheriff for Provo County.'

'You don't look like a sheriff,' said Alison. She sounded suspicious. The man was dressed in cut-off jeans and a faded T-shirt.

'These are my clothes for river patrol,' said the man. 'Even my stuffy boss doesn't insist that I go down the river in full uniform.'

'Boy, when you patrol your territory, you patrol,' said Jesse. 'Or is going down the river in a life jacket something you do for fun?'

'Neither,' said Sheriff Diamond. 'Although I'm pretty good in a kayak. Not good enough,' he added with a strange laugh.

Jody wondered if he were still in shock. Something about his story struck her as incoherent. She remembered what Jesse had told her about hypothermia. Maybe Sheriff Diamond was suffering from being in the cold water too long. His lips, although cracked and sunburned, did still look bluish, and he continued to shiver.

'I can tell my young saviour here thinks I've been in the water too long,' said Sheriff Diamond, again making that strange half-barking, half-laughing noise.

Then he started to cough and had to roll to the side. 'I

swallowed a little too much water,' he said, 'but I'm lucky to be alive. Didn't you guys read about the big prison escape we had two days ago?' he asked.

'We've been down in the canyon,' said Eric.

'Out of civilisation,' said Alison.

'Well, it's a good place to be out of,' said Sheriff Diamond. 'Though, come to think of it, that's how I got into this mess. I volunteered to come down here. Most people thought a private plane met the prisoner, but it occurred to me that you could take a jeep through Box Canyon and come down here. So I decided to check.'

'And you found him,' said Jody excitedly.

Sheriff Diamond shook his head sadly. 'No. If I had done that I wouldn't be so darned embarrassed. I just misread that rapids and turned over.'

Eric looked concerned. 'You mean you came down the river all by yourself – without a party?'

Sheriff Diamond turned his face away from Eric. 'Don't remind me how stupid I was, but I thought the canyons should be checked, and I knew the tourist season was starting so that other boats would be coming soon. Besides, it's not as if I haven't been riding Class Five waters ever since I was a kid. I've done all parts of the Snake, the River of No Return.'

Jesse gave him an admiring smile. 'All that and you went into law enforcement.'

Sheriff Diamond smiled back. 'I never wanted to mix up my hobby with my life, you know. I always liked living out on the edge.'

Eric still looked worried. 'What happened to your boat? And what kind was it?'

'I had a C-Two canoe. It was a custom job. I had added a centre cockpit so I could take it single, but I figured if I found Powell . . .'

'Who?' Jody asked.

'Pounding Pete Powell. He's the guy who escaped.'

'Pounding Pete?' repeated Jake. 'He sounds like a cartoon character – the dumb carpenter.'

'He's dumb, all right, but he got his name from liking to pound people's heads around.'

'Oh,' said Jake, 'well, that explains it.'

'Hardly,' said Jody. 'I thought you said several prisoners escaped. How come only one of you came down here? What would you have done if you caught them all?'

'I know Pounding Pete was the only one who knew his way around these canyons. He was an incredible white water canoer and kayaker.'

'I don't see your canoe. It must be downstream beyond the turn,' said Eric. 'Do you feel well enough to come with us while we look for it?'

'I'm fine,' said Sheriff Diamond. 'I think I hurt my pride more than anything else.'

Jody smiled. 'It's not easy to admit that,' she said.

'Well, it's true,' said Sheriff Diamond. He started to unravel himself from the sleeping bag Eric had given him to keep warm. 'If you ladies will excuse me, I'll get back into my clothes and then let's go. The best thing for me is to go back on the rapids.'

'Like getting back on a horse,' said Jake.

'Exactly. You have to get over your fear that you're going to capsize.' He grabbed his pack. 'At least I managed to salvage that. Which boat do you want me to take?'

'Take,' muttered Alison.

'I mean, ride in,' said Sheriff Diamond.

'He can ride with you – okay, Alison?' asked Eric.

'That would be fine,' said Alison. 'Why don't I go ahead with him and we can look for his boat. Maybe it's not damaged.'

'Okay,' said Eric. 'We'll follow right behind you.'

'Right,' said Alison, and she nodded curtly.

Jake started to climb into the raft.

'Where are you going, kid?' asked Matt Diamond.

'I'm in this boat,' answered Jake.

'Oh,' said Matt Diamond. He looked thoughtful.

'Is anything wrong?' asked Jake.

'No, no, kid,' said Matt Diamond. 'I was just thinking. Sorry. I must have got a little water in my brain. I still feel woozy.'

'Are you sure you feel well enough to go back into the rapids?' asked Jody.

Sheriff Diamond smiled at her. 'It takes more than one little dunk in the river to get me. I'm tough.'

'Let's get going,' said Alison.

9

BAD VIBES

About two hundred yards downriver Alison spotted something lodged between the rocks. 'I think that's your boat,' she shouted.

Expertly she guided the raft out of the tongue of the rapid and into the eddy where Matt's boat was caught. Matt leaped onto the shore and ran to his boat. He flipped it over.

Jake could see two holes about the size of basketballs in the canoe.

Matt kicked at the canoe furiously, making the holes bigger. He was so angry, he seemed out of control.

'What are you doing?' demanded Alison.

'It's ruined,' said Matt. His face had turned a deep purple.

'You're making sure of that,' said Alison.

Just then, Eric and Jesse guided their raft to the shore. 'You found it,' said Eric. 'It looks like it's in bad shape.'

'Completely ruined,' said Matt.

'Let me look at it,' said Eric. 'We have a repair kit with us. Maybe we can do something with it.'

'It's hopeless,' said Alison, who was bending over the canoe. 'He's right. A rock slashed through both sides.'

'It's part of the graveyard now,' said Matt. He sounded angry. 'I feel so stupid.'

'Everyone has accidents,' said Eric. 'Don't blame yourself. I'm just glad we happened to come through. It's a week before the tourist season really starts, you know. You could have been in awfully big trouble.'

'I could have been dead,' said Sheriff Diamond.

Jesse stared at him intently.

'Look,' said Eric, 'I think we've had enough excitement for the day. Why don't we make camp here? It's a good beach, and I was planning on stopping just a short way from here anyhow. We can use the rest.'

'Good idea,' said Jesse. He started to unload the rafts. He took out the big green garbage bag that held one night's dinner and the next morning's breakfast.

'It's my turn to cook,' said Alison. 'Give me that.'

'Gladly,' said Jesse, handing it to her.

'Jake, let's go find some wood,' said Jody.

'Do you need some more help?' asked Matt.

'No. You should rest,' said Jody. 'We can get enough.'

Matt smiled at them. 'I'm getting a couple of days of unearned vacation,' he said. 'Wait till my office hears that I happened to be picked up by a lovely young lady.'

'And a very competent woman river guide,' added Jake. 'Don't forget Alison.'

Alison was wrapping potatoes in aluminium foil. She didn't look up.

'I won't forget the lady river rat,' said Matt. 'By the way she manoeuvred us through the rapids this afternoon, I realised she could teach me a thing or two.'

'That's absolutely right,' said Alison sharply.

'Okay,' said Jake when they had got a little bit away from the others, 'what's wrong?'

'What do you mean, what's wrong?' asked Jody, picking up a large piece of twisted driftwood.

'You forget I'm your brother,' said Jake. 'I know you.

Something is bothering you. I knew it as soon as you said, "Jake, let's find some wood."'

'Now what's suspicious about asking you to get some wood?' demanded Jody.

'Nothing. But you get a clipped sound in your voice. I can always tell. Now what's bothering you? Jesse?'

'Jesse? What does he have to do with it?' asked Jody.

'I just thought the two of you were beginning to . . . you know,' stammered Jake. 'After all, he's good-looking enough. Even I can see that. Although I never thought you'd go for the daredevil type.'

Jake ducked as Jody tossed a piece of driftwood at him.

'Hey!' he shouted. 'I must be close or you wouldn't have tried to hit me.'

'I obviously wasn't trying very hard,' said Jody.

'Okay, what's upsetting you?' asked Jake.

'It's Matt,' said Jody. 'There's something about him that bothers me, only I can't figure out what it is.'

'Come off it, Jody, will you?' pleaded Jake. 'First your missing newspaper – now Matt. We're on vacation. We're not supposed to have to analyse everything. We've been through this before today. Stop dwelling on it. He's something of a character, but so what? I just don't want anything to ruin our good time.'

'You don't have to look at me as if I'm a party pooper,' said Jody, sounding hurt. 'I didn't make him fall out of his canoe.'

Jake looked instantly apologetic. 'I'm sorry. I guess I'm feeling sort of resentful that we have to take him along with us. The five of us seemed to be such a good group.'

'I know,' said Jody, 'and now the vibes feel different. Even Alison seems uptight.'

'What do you mean, "even Alison"?' asked Jake. 'She's terrific.'

'I didn't say anything against her,' said Jody. 'I like her too. Although maybe not as much as you do.'

Jake threw the piece of driftwood back at Jody.

Jody ducked. 'Now who doesn't like being teased?' she said. 'I thought you were getting a crush on Alison.'

Jake's sunburned face turned an even brighter red. 'I am not!' he protested. 'Besides, she's four years older than me.'

Jody laughed. 'Come on,' she said. 'You know nobody pays any attention to that stuff anymore.'

'I admire Alison,' said Jake stiffly. 'I do not have a crush on her.'

'I'm sorry,' said Jody. 'I hate it when you tease me. I don't know why I felt I had to tease you back.'

Jake's facial muscles seemed to relax. Every once in a while he was surprised by how much he and Jody could share.

'I'm sorry too,' he said. 'I guess without Mom to act as referee we have to be a little careful. Besides, I think you're right. We're all tense ever since we picked up Matt. The idea of an escaped convict in the canyon isn't very pleasant either.'

'I know,' said Jody. 'But I guess we'd better seriously gather wood or Eric and Jesse will come after us.'

Jody and Jake dragged their large pile of wood back to camp. Jesse and Eric were arguing. Matt sat on his haunches looking up at the two of them.

'You're running this like it's an army expedition,' yelled Jesse. 'I just want to scale the cliff. I've got my rope and climbing gear. The sun won't set for another few hours. What's the big deal?'

'And I say this was supposed to be a dry run for guests. What are you going to do when we're taking a tour down here. Are you just going to disappear?'

'Maybe some of them will want to climb. Jody wanted to last night, only you had to play the big leader,' retorted Jesse.

53

Jesse and Eric were so busy fighting they hadn't noticed that Jody and Jake had returned with their pile of wood.

Matt leaned back on his heels and glanced up at Jody and Jake. He grinned at them. 'They've been going after each other for the last fifteen minutes. Do they always work together so well?' he asked sarcastically.

'Oh, forget it,' said Jesse angrily. 'We'll do things your way. The safe way!' Jesse walked away.

Matt smiled as if he found Jesse very amusing.

'What are you grinning at?' asked Eric.

'Sorry,' said Matt. 'I was just thinking of why I like going downriver solo – although I don't mean to sound ungrateful. It's just that groups make me nervous.'

'It's not always this bad,' said Eric.

'Alison, do you need help with dinner?' asked Jake, hoping to break up the tension.

'No. Alison's famous glop is just about ready. Cheese, meat, dried mashed potatoes – add just the right amount of seasoning.'

Jake looked dubious. 'Maybe I'll cook tomorrow night,' he said.

'You're on,' said Eric quickly. 'Jake is one of the best natural cooks I know. If he ever wants to open a restaurant, I'll be a regular.'

'What about Jody?' asked Matt. 'If my little saviour is a good cook, maybe I'll marry her.'

'Maybe she won't want to,' snapped Jody.

'I was only joking,' said Matt. 'I'm not the kind to rob the cradle.'

'The joke was in bad taste,' said Jesse, glaring at Matt.

'Speaking of taste,' said Alison in a high voice that almost sounded like a falsetto. She giggled and suddenly looked very girlish and young. 'Is anyone interested in some glop?' Alison was trying to break the odd tension between everybody.

'Now, how can anyone refuse an invitation like that?' said Jake, handing his metal cup to Alison. Jake took a bite.

'What's your verdict?' asked Alison. 'Or maybe I should ask you not to munchon it.'

'The trouble with you as a cook, Alison,' said Jake, 'is that you're always pudding us on.'

Eric groaned and held out his cup. 'Well, it can't be so bad if it's got the two of you punning again.'

'Actually this glop tastes good,' said Jake. Alison grinned at him.

10

DEATH TO
ALL SCORPIONS!

Jody awoke to the sound of the river. She looked across the canyon. The shapes and swirls of the rocks looked too fantastical to be anything other than the work of a mad artist. The very tips of the spirals were dipped in red from the sunrise.

Jody felt privileged and happy to be allowed to see the world from the bottom of the canyon. With no other people around except their little group, she felt alone but not lonely. She sat up in her sleeping bag and looked around. Everyone else seemed to be sleeping. Somehow being the only one awake made Jody feel even more privileged. She imagined that one day Butch Cassidy himself might have slept on the very spot where she was sleeping. He would have awakened early, tense because a posse was following him. He would have splashed cold water on his face from the river. His eyes would have glanced up to the rim of the canyon, thousands of feet above him, and tried to judge how close the posse might be.

Jody climbed out of her sleeping bag, determined to go to the river and splash cold water on *her* face. She tried to remember what she knew of female outlaws. There was Belle Starr, who had ridden with the Younger Brothers. She wondered if Belle had ever used the river as an escape route. Jody decided to switch her fantasy from Butch Cassidy to Belle Starr.

She got her sneakers out of their bag. Then she remembered that in all the Westerns she had seen, cowboys always shook out their boots in the morning. Even though her sneakers had been in her plastic bag, she decided to go on with her fantasy. She turned her sneaker upside down. Then she screamed.

A scorpion fell out onto her lap. It looked like a tiny earth-brown lobster. Its small pincers opened and shut as if winking at Jody. Its long tail curled up. Jody knew that if she tried to jump up, it could sting her before she moved. She knew the dangerous-looking pincers were actually innocent. Its tail held all the poison, but that poison could kill.

Jody held her breath. She didn't want to scream again. The scorpion was crawling slowly across her lap. If she screamed she'd have to take a breath and that might disturb the insect. Luckily she had slept in her jeans. Jody had to command herself not to shudder as she thought of what might have happened had she gone to sleep as she usually did in just a T-shirt.

'Jody!' whispered a voice above her. 'Why did you scream?'

Jody recognised Jesse's voice. Carefully Jody nodded her head so that Jesse could see the scorpion in her lap.

'Oh, my God,' hissed Jesse. 'Don't move.'

'Get him off me,' pleaded Jody.

Jesse got a stick from the pile by the fire.

'Don't try to kill him – just sweep him off me,' whispered Jody. She knew that if Jesse tried to kill the scorpion and missed, the insect would sting her in self-defence.

Quickly Jesse used the stick like a broom. The scorpion fell on its back on a rock to the side of Jody's sleeping bag. It waved its pincers back and forth angrily.

'Be careful!' commanded Jody. Jesse was standing over the scorpion with his stick held high.

'What's happening?' Matt asked.

Jody didn't answer. She took a large rock, making sure that it was much larger than the scorpion. She gestured for Jesse to get out of the way in case she missed. Then she slammed the rock down hard on the scorpion.

Jesse ran up and put his arms around her shoulders. 'Quick thinking,' he said. 'Are you all right?'

Jody looked down at her hands. They were shaking. 'It was in my sneaker,' she said, her voice trembling. 'I was about to put my foot in when I shook him out.'

'Thank goodness you shook it,' said Alison.

'Why didn't you put your sneakers in your bag?' demanded Eric.

'I did,' protested Jody, close to tears. 'I don't know how it got in there.'

'You must not have closed it tight,' said Jesse. 'It's a good thing I was there when you woke up.'

'What were you doing up so early?' asked Alison.

'I . . . uh,' said Jesse, seemingly startled.

'Never mind that,' said Matt. 'How did you happen to find the scorpion before you put your shoe on? It seems to me you were mighty lucky.'

Jody blushed. 'I was pretending I was Belle Starr, and in the movies the outlaws always shake out their boots.'

'Thank goodness,' said Alison, her voice full of relief.

'As Matt says,' added Jesse, 'you're awfully lucky.'

'I don't understand how the scorpion got in, though,' said Jody. 'I did close my bag tight.'

'They can get in anything when they want to,' said Jesse.

'Do you feel all right now, Jody? You had a close call.'

'I know,' said Jody. 'Would I have died from the bite?'

'Not necessarily,' said Eric, 'but you could have been very sick. Probably we would have had to send one raft ahead to get help and some of us would have stayed with you.'

'Don't we have medicine for scorpion bites?' asked Alison.

'Of course,' said Eric, 'but you know as well as I do that you can't predict how the medicine works or if the person is going to react to the bite. Some people are more susceptible than others.'

'Then it could have killed her, couldn't it?' said Jake, sounding more and more horrified.

'Let's not get morbid. Let's just eat breakfast and we'll get back on the river,' said Eric curtly.

Everyone seemed on edge. Only Sheriff Diamond sounded relaxed. 'I remember once I was going down Big Drop when I noticed I had a scorpion riding with me. I tell you, I almost took a tumble and lost everything.'

Alison muttered something.

'What did you say?' asked Sheriff Diamond.

'Nothing,' said Alison. 'I'm going to help Eric with breakfast.'

Alison and Eric made pancakes. They were delicious, but Jody only picked at her food.

'Come on, Jody, cheer up,' said Matt. 'Just because you executed a scorpion is no reason to get the blues. In fact, you should feel good about it. The only good scorpion is a dead scorpion.'

'I don't really believe that,' said Jody. 'Scorpions lived here before we did. Scorpions probably lived here at the same time the dinosaurs wandered around this land. I had no right to kill it.'

'It was kill or be killed,' said Matt. 'Don't tell me you're one of those bleeding-heart liberals who can't kill a fly.'

'She obviously isn't like that,' said Jesse. 'You saw the way she handled that scorpion. Splat!'

'Besides,' said Jody angrily, 'I don't see what being a bleeding-heart liberal has to do with anything. I don't think every liberal has a "bleeding-heart".'

'Please, no arguments about politics,' pleaded Alison. 'I've seen too many trips ruined when passengers got into fights about politics.'

'I agree,' said Eric.

'Me too,' said Matt. 'But if you ask me, all scorpions should be taken before a firing squad and shot, like we execute people in Utah. No questions asked.'

'Nobody asked you,' snapped Alison.

'I can just see it now,' said Jake. 'You could get army ants to do the executing.'

'I don't think it's funny,' said Jody. 'And for the record, I am not a bleeding-heart and I do not believe in capital punishment. The state can make a mistake, and the government should not be in the business of taking lives.'

'I thought we were agreed that we wouldn't talk politics,' said Eric.

'I'm sorry,' said Jody. 'I didn't mean to get on a soapbox. I just had to say what I believe.'

'Listen, I respect you for it,' said Matt. 'I didn't mean to pick a fight. Just because I like the state of Utah and believe in the firing squad and you don't, it doesn't mean we can't be friends. That's what makes horse races. Some states prefer the electric chair or the gas chamber. I always liked Utah for keeping to old-fashioned ways.'

'Enough!' demanded Alison.

Matt looked embarrassed. He held his hand out to Jody. 'Friends?' he asked ingratiatingly.

Jody gave him her hand. 'Friends,' she answered.

11

A GAME GIRL!

'Well, Jody, this is it,' said Jesse. 'This is where we separate the men from the boys.'

Jody gave him a wry look. 'I guess that leaves me out,' she said.

'Whoops!' said Jesse. 'I didn't mean to say that.'

They were back in the rafts, about to go through the biggest rapids of the trip. So far the river had been dropping about five feet per mile. Now it would start dropping more than thirty feet per mile.

Jody felt the adrenaline pump through her bloodstream. She and Matt and Jesse were in one raft. Alison, Eric, and Jake were in the other.

'I can hear it!' shouted Matt.

The river growled at them as it rushed by.

'This is the way I like it!' shouted Jesse. 'When you just run the river and take what it gives you.'

'Me too!' shouted Matt. His eyes gleamed with excitement.

'Let's just hope it doesn't give us too much!' said Jody.

Jesse handed Jody a bailing bucket. 'Get ready!' he said.

Jody tightened the ring on her life jacket.

The river dashed back and forth at the rocks, as if furious that they were in the way. Jesse knifed the oar blade into the wave's fat crest and pulled with all his might, slipping past first one rock and then the other.

Ragged waves crashed down on Jody and Jake as they bailed with all their might. Jody forgot about the canyon's walls, forgot about everything else except looking ahead to try to warn Jesse and Matt of rocks treacherously hidden under too little water or thrashing holes that could turn into whirlpools that would trap the raft.

Suddenly there was time to think again and the world of sky and cliffs and colours existed again. They looked behind them. Eric's raft came bobbing up. Eric made a thumbs-up gesture, congratulating Jesse on the way he had run the river.

They looked ahead. There was a long sandbar reaching down toward the head of the rapid and slanted up from the river to jumbled rocks overlooking it.

'Let's land over there!' shouted Eric.

'No!' shouted Jesse. 'We ran that one perfectly. Let's just keep going.'

'Don't be stupid, Jesse. We are not going to run Big Drop without scouting it. Pull in!' Eric commanded.

Jesse shrugged his shoulders. 'Your cousin sure is the cautious type.'

'Why do you always have to fight Eric?' Jody asked.

'I don't,' said Jesse defensively. Then he seemed to think about it. 'I guess maybe I do. Maybe I'm jealous that Eric's the leader.'

'But you seem to like people calling you a daredevil,' said Jody.

Jesse winked at Jody. His bright blue eyes gave nothing away of what he was thinking.

They landed on the sandbar. Matt got out of the raft and stretched his legs.

'Were you scared?' he asked.

'Not really,' said Jody. 'You and Jesse seem to know what you're doing.'

'You're such a game girl,' said Matt.

Jody loosened her life jacket. She turned to Jake. 'Come on. Let's explore a little while they're studying the rapids.' They picked their way over the rocks and driftwood. 'Game girl!' muttered Jody.

'Something tells me that Matt Diamond is getting on your nerves,' said Jake.

'What makes you think that?' snapped Jody. 'Just because he insists on calling me "little girl"?'

'Oh, come on,' said Jake. 'He's not that bad.'

'I know,' said Jody.

Eric signalled to them. Jody and Jake climbed down to join them. 'It looks pretty awesome, doesn't it?' he said, pointing down the river.

'There doesn't seem to be room between the rocks,' said Jody.

'That's why it's a good thing we looked first,' said Eric, nodding pointedly at Jesse. 'Do you see those rocks nearly hidden? From a boat we wouldn't have been able to see them until we were nearly on top, and they could rip our raft to shreds.'

'We call them sleepers,' said Alison. 'No pun intended, but if you hit one you can go to sleep for a long time.'

'We're going to have to try to shoot right down the middle of the tail,' said Jesse, 'and pull hard left in order not to get tangled up in those rocks.'

'What would happen if there wasn't a way to get through?' asked Jody.

'We'd have to portage,' said Jesse. 'That's what John Wesley Powell had to do. You carry all your stuff around the rocks. Sometimes they would line the boats, haul them through the river with ropes. It's hard work.'

'I bet,' said Jake.

'Hey, Eric, as long as we're stopped here, shouldn't we show Jody and Jake the Anasazi Indian caves?' said Alison.

'Caves?' said Jake excitedly. 'What caves?'

'There were Indians who lived in these canyons in the tenth and eleventh centuries,' said Eric. 'They were gradually driven from the more fertile land above us until they hid out here. They scratched out a living. Their caves are right up there.'

Eric pointed up the canyon wall about three hundred feet. Jody shielded her eyes against the sun. She could just make out a series of indentations high up on the rocks.

'Let's go and see them,' said Jody.

'Actually, they're quite interesting,' said Alison.

'Do you want to come with us?' asked Jody.

'No,' said Alison. 'I have some chores to do around here.'

'Doesn't anyone want to come?' asked Jake.

The four each looked at one another. Jody felt as if there was a strange tension, but she couldn't understand whom it was coming from. 'I want to dry out our sleeping bags,' said Eric. 'They got splashed in that last rapid. But we'll rest here an hour or two.'

'Come on, Jody,' said Jake. 'It's the two of us. We're off to see the caves.'

'Just watch out for scorpions,' said Jesse.

'Don't worry,' said Jody. 'One run-in with a scorpion is enough.'

'Besides,' said Jesse, 'if it's excitement you crave, we've still got the rapids that John Wesley Powell named Satan's Gut ahead of us.'

12

NIGHTMARE IN MIDDAY

Jody and Jake had filled their canteens with fresh water and dipped their shirts in the river before beginning their climb. They each wore work shirts and cut-off jeans over their bathing suits. They had been climbing only fifteen minutes before their shirts were already dry and stiff from the sun.

Jake looked up the cliff toward the caves. 'Somehow they seem to be getting farther away instead of closer,' he said.

'That's just because we have to climb at an angle,' said Jody. 'You can't just walk straight up a sheer cliff.'

'I think I know why the others didn't want to come,' said Jake.

Every once in a while as they climbed they came upon a pine tree that had found a crevice full of soil and taken root. Seen from the river level they looked like toy trees no more than an inch high, but actually the trees were thirty and forty feet tall.

Jody stopped by one of the trees. She hung on to its branches and looked down at the river.

'Find a resting spot?' Jake asked.

'It's just so beautiful,' said Jody, looking at the glowing, eye-smarting reds of sandstone, the bright white lines of limestone. 'I wish I knew more geology. I'll have to ask Eric to teach me.'

'I wish I knew how much farther it is to the caves,' said Jake, taking a sip from his canteen.

'Don't drink that too fast,' said Jody. 'It's got to last us the rest of the way up and down.'

'I wonder what the Indians lived on up here,' said Jake. 'They had to get water from somewhere.'

'Let's go on,' said Jody.

'Hey, wait a minute!' shouted Jake. 'Do you see what I see!'

Far below them a raft bobbed between the huge boulders. Four people were in it.

'It must be another party,' said Jody. 'Funny that we didn't know they were so close to us.'

'Jody——' stammered Jake. 'I saw long hair. It looks like Alison. But it couldn't be, could it?'

'Of course not,' said Jody. 'They wouldn't have gone without us. It's just such a shock to see other people. Somehow down in the canyon we've had the feeling that we are the only people in the world.'

Jake watched the small raft round a bend in the river and disappear. *'Alison! Jesse!'* he shouted.

'Alison! Jesse!' echoed back from the canyon walls. Jake's voice bounced back and forth across the canyon and then faded. Jody and Jake were left in silence except for the ever-present sound of the roaring river.

Jake stared at his sister.

'Maybe they didn't hear you,' said Jody, but her own voice was unsteady.

'Jody, they could have heard me in California,' said Jake.

Jody cupped her hands to her mouth. *'Jesse! Eric! Alison!'* she shouted.

Her voice bounced back and forth across the walls. Her

voice bounced back at a higher pitch than Jake's had. But when Jody's echo faded, nobody answered.

'Let's go down there,' said Jody grimly.

'They wouldn't have left us here,' said Jake. 'There's got to be some mistake. You must be right. Somehow they didn't hear us yell.'

'You're right,' said Jody, and then she smiled in relief. 'The river!'

'What about the river?' asked Jake doubtfully.

'The river does strange things to echoes,' said Jody confidently. 'We hear it so loud up here, down there it must drown out all other sounds. We forgot we were up high. That's why they didn't hear us.'

'So you don't think that was them we saw go down the river?' asked Jake, his voice still trembling.

'Absolutely not,' said Jody. 'We'd have to be paranoid to think that. Let's turn around and go back up to the caves. They must be just behind us.'

'Right,' said Jake. 'We would look pretty silly panicking and thinking that somehow they had abandoned us.'

'Yeah,' agreed Jody. She giggled. 'They'd think we had rocks in our heads.'

Jake reached out and put his hand on a big black rock. 'That's right,' he said. 'And you know what happens to rocks that have been around a long time?'

'No,' said Jody suspiciously.

'They get taken for granite,' said Jake.

'Maybe you should have waited for Alison to tell that one,' said Jody.

'She's the one who told it to me,' said Jake.

'Jake,' said Jody, 'I feel funny. It does seem so weirdly silent.'

'I know,' said Jake. 'Let's go back down and look for them. So what if they think we're paranoid. I'll feel better. Seeing that raft go down the river gave me the creepiest feeling.'

'Me too,' said Jody, glad that she and Jake were not trying to fool each other any more.

They scrambled down the path, both finding it harder to go down the rocks than it had been to climb up. Despite the dry air, Jody's back was wet with sweat and her shirt clung to her.

The farther they got back down the canyon wall, the more Jody felt herself panic. Except for the sound of the river, there was still no other sound. She and Jake should have been able to hear Eric, Jesse, Matt, and Alison talking. While it was possible to imagine Eric working quietly, Jesse, Alison, and Matt were all three so volatile that Jody couldn't believe they would be together and *not* talk.

Jody looked at her watch. She and Jake had left the others almost forty-five minutes ago. Time enough for them to have put out all the sleeping bags to dry and to have started up. With each step down the path, Jody felt her heart beating faster, as if what she feared could be true.

'Jody, it's awfully quiet,' said Jake.

Jody nodded. They had reached a corner in the path, and now they were directly above the sandbar where they had left the others. It was deserted.

Something dark and grey, like an old blanket, lay on the beach. Jody ran to it. A look of horror flashed over her face. She held up the grey mass to Jake.

It was one of the rafts, slashed into ribbons – not merely beyond repair, but attacked again and again with a knife, as if someone had been taking out his or her fury at the raft.

'It can't be,' whispered Jake.

13

ABANDONED!

Jody paced back and forth on the sand spit.

'You're making me dizzy,' complained Jake.

'I'm thinking,' answered Jody. She didn't stop pacing.

'I think it had to be a snakebite,' said Jake. 'One of them got bitten by a snake. No – if it was just one of them, they would have left one person to wait for us. Two of them got bitten by a snake and they needed to rip up the raft for tourniquets.'

'Jake, you're babbling,' said Jody.

'I know,' said Jake, 'but it keeps me from getting hysterical. I feel like shrieking *Help!*'

'Shriek,' said Jody.

'*Help!*' screamed Jake at the top of his lungs. His voice bounced off the canyon walls and back at him, almost as if his own voice were mocking him. When the echoes had died away, he turned and looked at Jody. 'We've really been abandoned, haven't we?' he said sadly. 'Nobody even left us a note.'

Jody nodded. 'I don't trust Matt,' she said. 'Somehow he's behind the fact that we've been abandoned. In fact, I'm convinced that he is the escaped killer he claimed he was searching for.'

'Jody,' said Jake, 'you've got no proof.'

Jody paced in tighter and tighter circles. 'It's the only explanation we have to work with. Something has been bothering me about Matt all day. I finally figured it out. In Utah, if you're condemned to death, you get to choose between the electric chair and the firing squad,' said Jody.

Jake sat up and did a double take. 'I feel like I've fallen into a rabbit hole. You're talking like a weird Alice in Wonderland. What do firing squads and electric chairs have to do with anything?'

'When Matt and I got into an argument about capital punishment, he said something about all killers should be put before a firing squad like they do in Utah. A real law enforcement official from Utah would have mentioned that condemned killers get a choice. But if you were a killer yourself, and you had decided you wanted to be shot before a firing squad, you probably wouldn't have mentioned it.' Jody looked puzzled. 'At least, I think that's what you would do.'

'How did you happen to know about Utah's law?' asked Jake.

'I did a report on Gary Gilmore,' said Jody. 'Look, I'm not saying I'm absolutely right, but just suppose I am. Everything would make sense. Matt Diamond is an escaped killer. He takes my newspaper because he doesn't want us to see his picture. He somehow gets hold of a canoe and tries to make it down the river, figuring he'd get out of Utah and hide out in Arizona. He has an accident and suddenly gets picked up by five strangers. He makes up a story that he's the sheriff, and he tries to improvise a way out. First, he tries to get rid of me by putting a scorpion in my shoe.'

'Why would he do that?' asked Jake.

'I had the newspaper,' said Jody, getting more and more excited as she talked. 'He knew I would recognise him from the article. Then, when that didn't work, he got rid of us. Although I don't understand how he got all of them to go along with him.'

'Maybe he had a gun in his pack,' said Jake. 'Remember? He held on to his pack awfully carefully.'

'That must be it,' said Jody, although she still looked perplexed, as if something was bothering her.

Jake looked up. 'Meanwhile, they're down the river with a gun in their backs and we're stuck here. There's nothing we can do to help them.'

Jody looked at her watch. It was 5:30. Soon the sun would be making its way down the canyon walls.

'You're right,' she said. 'There's nothing we can do tonight. We've got to find a place to sleep.'

'I don't think I like the sound of that "tonight",' said Jake 'It implies that tomorrow morning you think we can do something.'

'Let's worry about tomorrow tomorrow,' said Jody. 'Come on, let's go find those Indian caves.'

'This is no time to go exploring,' protested Jake.

'I'm not talking about exploring,' said Jody. 'Somehow the Indians found the secret of surviving up there. Maybe we will too. At any rate, we'll have shelter for the night.'

Jody and Jake climbed several hundred feet above the river. The steep shale cliff occasionally crumbled beneath them as they climbed. Every time Jake tried to talk to Jody she cut him off sharply. They made their trek in absolute silence. Finally they reached several little rectangular rock slab rooms set into the cliff in an L shape.

'They aren't very homely,' said Jake, kicking away some of the shale that had come loose on the bottom of the cave.

'I know,' said Jody, 'but let's gather some wood. I want to look around above here.'

Several pine trees were growing out from the canyon wall

at forty-degree angles. Several pine cones and dead branches lay underneath the trees. Jody gathered them up and brought them into the cave.

'Terrific,' said Jake. 'Are we going to sleep on them, or are we going to rub two sticks together to start a fire?'

'No. But we'd better wait until the last moment. Pine burns hot, but fast. It won't last very long.'

'I see,' said Jake. 'But you do plan on lighting it?'

'Yes,' said Jody. 'I'll show you how later. We're not as helpless as they think.'

'I see,' said Jake sarcastically. 'And now I suppose you've got an answer for what we're going to eat and drink while we're waiting. Probably you think the Indians left some freeze-dried deer meat waiting for me to whip into a stew.'

'I wish getting food could be so easy. But we can survive without food a lot longer than we can without water.' Jody left the cave and started climbing up the canyon wall.

'Could you please tell me what you're doing?' pleaded Jake. 'You're making me more nervous being abandoned with *you* than I might be all by myself.'

Jody looked down at her brother. 'I'm sorry,' she said suddenly.

'You're treating me as if I'm some stranger,' said Jake. 'I don't know what you're thinking.'

Jody's face softened. 'Jake, I'm sorry. It's been such a shock and I'm scared – scared for us and even more frightened for them.'

Jake took a deep breath. 'You were giving me commands like you were a general.'

'I'm just as upset as you,' said Jody. 'And scared. But I figure if the Indians could survive up here a few hundred years ago, we probably can too. They must have had a fresh water source or they wouldn't have chosen to live here. The Colorado is too dirty to drink, and I'm afraid it's polluted.

There are more trees growing up here than down by the river. There's got to be fresh water.'

'Now *that* makes sense,' said Jake. 'If you had told me I wouldn't have had such a fit. I almost threw you down into the river when we were walking up here.'

'And every time you even breathed I was getting mad,' said Jody. 'I think we were both feeling so crazy we wanted to take it out on each other.'

Jake looked at his sister. 'The thing is, when we talk about it I feel better.'

'I know,' said Jody, 'but I feel I need to mull it over in my head before we talk.'

'And when you're quiet and we're in a tough place, it drives me crazy!' said Jake, his voice rising.

'And that's why we're such a good pair,' said Jody.

14

A NIGHT IN A CAVE

'All right,' said Jake. 'I'm waiting for you to pull off your miracle.' He looked down at the wood Jody had gathered. 'Somehow you're going to get it lit.'

'I helped us find water, didn't I?' said Jody. Jody's instincts had been right. The Indians had chosen their home well. Only a few feet from their caves Jody had found a spring of cool, fresh water. The two had emptied their canteens of the now stale water and drunk heavily. Then they refilled their canteens and retreated back to the Indian caves as the canyon grew dark. Already the river below them was completely in shadows, but the sun's last rays shone into the cave.

'I hope you're not really expecting me to rub some sticks together,' said Jake, 'because I flunked out of the Boy Scouts.'

'You didn't flunk out. You quit,' said Jody. 'You were interested in other things. But I was a Girl Guide until I was thirteen.' Jody reached in her pocket and pulled out a piece of glass. 'Remember when I broke the mirror? One of the pieces wasn't sharp and I put it in my pocket. Let's hope it works.'

Jake watched as Jody angled her piece of mirror so that it caught the sun's rays. 'It always worked at Girl Guide camp,' said Jody. 'I was amazed that it worked just like in the movies.'

'Let's hope it works now,' said Jake. 'Maybe if it works it will break the spell of seven years' bad luck, although so far I'd say that superstition is true.'

'We'd better hurry,' said Jody. 'That sun is setting fast.'

Jody and Jake stared at the little pile of twigs as if willing it to catch fire from the sun's concentrated rays. Jody kept making minute changes in the angle with which she held the mirror. Then suddenly Jake saw a tiny wisp of smoke.

'It's working,' he cried. He was so happy that tears came to his eyes. He hugged Jody. Jody hugged him back. Soon they had a blazing fire to warm themselves and it made their fear recede.

'Now we've got fire and water,' said Jake. 'You don't have a candy bar in your pocket too?'

'Don't worry about food,' said Jody. 'Just keep telling yourself that you can survive without food for weeks.'

'I'm not sure that I want to survive without food,' said Jake. 'I'm hungry already, and so far we haven't even missed one meal.'

'Don't think about food,' said Jody.

'That's like asking the river not to think about going downhill,' said Jake morosely.

'Don't you know any river jokes?' asked Jody, poking the fire.

'You must really be worried about cheering me up,' said Jake.

'What do you call the little rivers that run into the Nile?' asked Jody.

Jake could see an unusual half-smile on Jody's face. 'I don't know,' he answered quizzically.

'Juveniles!' said Jody triumphantly.

'Did you just make that up,' asked Jake, 'or did you hear it somewhere?'

'I'm not telling,' said Jody.

'Come on,' said Jake. 'I'll confess to you. Sometimes I think up a pun and then I wait for a chance to use it in a conversation. I don't think them all up spontaneously. Sometimes I don't make them up. I hear them from other kids or on TV or I read them somewhere.'

'I've got a confession too,' said Jody. 'I never thought you did make them all up on the spot.'

Jake squirmed around on the hard floor of the cave trying to find a comfortable position. 'This is no place for deathbed confessions,' he said. 'Actually it would be a cave-bed confession. I wonder if the Indians who lived here went hungry at night. Maybe this cave is haunted by hungry Indians.'

'Actually, I'm afraid that on most nights the Indians who lived here went hungry,' said Jody. 'The only reason they lived here was that more powerful Indians kept forcing them into retreat.'

'I knew it!' said Jake. 'All night I'll probably be haunted by hungry Indians.' Suddenly Jake tried to stand up and cracked his head against the roof of the cave. 'Hungry *short* Indians at that.'

'They were probably short because they didn't get enough to eat,' said Jody. 'Malnutrition does that to you.'

'See? I'll probably shrink.' Jake sighed. 'Jody, are we just talking to make ourselves feel better?'

'Partly,' said Jody. She paused. 'We're scared,' she admitted.

'We've been in scary situations before,' said Jake, 'but this feels so different. It's like falling into a science fiction story. At one moment you're with friends in a normal situation; the next minute your friends abandon you to survive in the wilderness and you think one of your friends is an escaped killer. You didn't set this up, did you? This isn't one of those survival tests like Outward Bound that's supposed to make a man out of a juvenile delinquent?'

'What is it with being in the wilderness?' said Jody. 'That is the second time I've heard somebody say something will make a man out of me.'

'The wilderness just brings out the macho in all of us brutes,' said Jake. 'Wow! If Mom could hear me now, she'd spank me.'

'If you don't cut it out, I'll spank you. Let's go to sleep.'

'How?' asked Jake. 'We're lying on a rocky ledge. We've got nothing to cover ourselves. I've never gone to sleep without at least a sheet over me.'

'It'll make a man out of you,' said Jody, joking.

Jake gave her a dirty look. 'I feel like we're in prison,' said Jake.

'In our prisons they give you a blanket and a bed,' said Jody. 'Of course——' Jody's voice drifted off.

The fire was dying now. Jake leaned back against the rocky wall of their home. It was a square room, chipped out painstakingly by Indians hundreds of years ago. The rocks felt sharp and uncomfortable. He lay down, curling himself into a ball. 'I feel like an animal,' he said.

'We are animals,' said Jody. 'But only human animals get themselves in these predicaments.' Jody's voice sounded edgy and bitter.

15

JODY'S FEARS

Jake opened his eyes and instantly he remembered exactly where he was. He uncurled himself and sat up. His body felt as if he'd been playing football against the Buffalo Bills' defensive line and he hadn't been wearing any padding. He looked around the cave. It was empty.

'Jody!' he cried, his voice full of alarm.

'I'm here!' said Jody.

Jake stepped out of the cave. Jody had climbed up to the crack in the canyon wall where they had found the stream. She grinned down at Jake.

'Will you stop pretending you're Mary Poppins?' said Jake grumpily. Usually he was the one who woke up wide awake and talkative, but their emergency seemed to bring out a new early-morning Jody. Jake looked at his watch. It was 5:30 A.M. 'What are you doing up?' he demanded.

'I couldn't sleep,' said Jody. She climbed down and stood next to Jake. Now that she was closer, Jake could see that she had dark circles under her eyes, and she didn't look quite as impossibly cheery as he had first thought.

'I couldn't stand watching you sleep,' said Jody. 'I kept shifting my position trying to get comfortable and there you were, snoring.'

'I don't snore,' objected Jake.

'How would you know?' asked Jody. 'You were asleep. You slept like you were back home in bed.'

'Well, it's not my fault,' said Jake, who suddenly felt guilty that he had slept well, as if somehow he wasn't taking their predicament seriously enough. Furthermore, his stomach was growling. 'I'm hungry,' said Jake.

'Can't you stop talking about food for one moment?' shouted Jody.

Jake sat down by the edge of their cave and looked down at the river. Tears formed in the corners of his eyes. He felt scared, hungry, and angry.

Jody sat down next to him. Jake glanced over at her, ashamed to let her see him crying. To his surprise, Jody was crying too. Jake realised that he could count on one hand the times that he had seen Jody cry.

'How come we didn't cry last night when it was even more frightening,' sniffled Jake.

'Because it was too scary to cry last night,' said Jody. 'I was afraid that if I started to cry last night, I might never stop. That's why I got so mad when I had to listen to you snoring. I'm sorry I snapped at you.'

'Forget it,' said Jake. He looked back down at the river again. 'What do you think is happening with the others? You don't think Matt would kill them, do you? He wouldn't be able to handle all three of them. Somehow with three against one, they're bound to find a way to get free.'

'I don't think it is three against one,' said Jody slowly. 'That's what I was thinking about last night. My newspaper got stolen before we picked up Matt Diamond. Somehow in our panic about being abandoned I forgot that.'

'So what?' asked Jake. 'What does it matter when your newspaper got stolen?' Then Jake gasped. He suddenly realised what Jody was saying. 'You mean that one of our group knew Matt . . .'

'It had to be,' said Jody. 'Matt had just escaped from prison. How could he have got hold of a canoe unless someone helped him? Someone didn't want us to think about the prison escape. They took my newspaper, and then when we caught up with Matt they worked with him.'

'But who?' asked Jake. 'You can't suspect Eric. He's our cousin. Alison wouldn't do it. I like her. That leaves Jesse.'

'It could be any of them,' said Jody. 'Eric is our cousin, but it's possible he could know Matt somehow. Just because he's our cousin, it doesn't leave him out. Eric is an experienced rafter and outfitter. He's in charge. He could have got hold of a canoe to give Matt. Suppose Matt is his best friend from college. We don't know anything about Eric's life in college. As for Alison, she's been edgy ever since we picked up Matt.'

'But so have you, for that matter,' said Jake.

'As for Jesse, he was standing near me when I woke up with the scorpion in my shoe. He saw the newspaper first. He's a daredevil. We all know that. I admit he's the most likely suspect.'

Jake took a rock and flung it toward the river. 'This is frustrating! It's driving me crazy. We're stuck here, and we have to speculate about which one of our friends is helping a killer. Maybe the sun has got to us and none of this is true. They're in a boat; we're on foot. How could we possibly catch up with them?' argued Jake.

'Maybe we can't,' said Jody, 'but we've got to try. It's two against two. If we do catch up with them, we can even up the odds. It's worth taking the chance. Remember, he has a gun.'

'It sure seems like a long shot to me,' said Jake. 'But let's go.' He stood up. 'Anything is better than just sitting here helpless.'

Jody and Jake picked their way back down to the river. Jody stopped short. The shoreline was a jumble of boulders. The river growled at them and rushed on below them, leaving almost no room to walk around. Jody and Jake felt the spray from the huge waves on their faces.

'There's got to be a way around this rapid,' said Jody.

'That's the spirit!' said Jake. 'Never say die. Unfortunately, I think the Colorado has even more spirit than you do.'

Jody scowled at the river that blocked her path. 'The Indians who lived in those caves, must have had a path,' she said.

Jake looked up at the cliffs. 'How about if we climbed up instead of down?' asked Jake. 'Maybe there's a town up there that we don't even know about. A town with telephones. We could call Mom and get out of this mess.'

'No,' said Jody. 'Two of John Wesley Powell's men did that and they were the only ones who got killed. They were shot by Indians.'

Jake stared at his sister. 'I don't think we have to worry about being shot by Indians,' he said. 'Besides, you pick up the oddest bits of information.'

'I can't help it,' said Jody. 'I've got a good memory for odd facts.'

'I'd call it an odd memory and leave it at that,' said Jake. 'But John Wesley Powell's men were here over a hundred years ago. I still think we should consider climbing up and out over the canyon walls. They're high, but we should be able to make it by nightfall and we could get help.'

'You're dreaming,' said Jody. 'We're over a mile in here without fresh water, and our canteens wouldn't carry enough for us to make it. We'd die of dehydration. At least if we stay down here by the river we can drink the river water. It's silty and dirty and it might make us sick, but we'd survive.'

'I guess you're right,' said Jake, looking down at the churning water. 'But I don't see how we're going to catch up when we can barely make it around these rapids.'

81

'Wait a minute,' said Jody. 'What's that? Do you see something hanging from that tree?'

Jody pointed to a tree hanging out over the river about fifty yards downstream. Hanging from its branches seemed to be two large orange flowers, almost as large as balloons.

'No tree has flowers that large,' said Jody.

Jake squinted downstream. The sun had crept down the canyon walls and here and there shafts of sunlight lit the river.

'Desert flowers are weird,' said Jake.

'That's no desert flower,' said Jody. 'It's life jackets.'

'Come on, Jody,' said Jake, sounding worried. 'The desert has got to you. You're starting to have delusions – like one of those mirages. We need life jackets and *wham-o*, you see life jackets growing on trees.'

'I tell you those are life jackets!' said Jody. 'Someone hoped that we would follow. Someone must have found a moment to fling those life jackets out.'

'I hope whoever did it isn't in trouble,' said Jake.

'I know,' said Jody. 'We've got to hope that Matt and his accomplice think that the others are worth more to them alive than dead. Otherwise, they'll kill them.'

'If they had wanted hostages, why would they have abandoned us?' asked Jake.

'I don't know,' said Jody. 'That puzzles me. But one step at a time. Let's get those life jackets first.'

16

A DARING RISK

'I wish I had a rope,' said Jody.

Jake looked at the wild river. 'Jody,' he said seriously. 'I don't think we should risk our lives for those life jackets. It's too dangerous. I'm not joking.'

'I know,' said Jody. 'But even if there's one chance in a thousand that we can catch up with them, we've got to take it. Someone could get killed if we don't reach them.'

'*If* you're right,' said Jake. 'So far all we've been doing is speculating. It could turn out that there's another explanation entirely.'

'Do you want to take that chance?' asked Jody.

Jake shrugged his shoulders. He sighed. 'I guess you're right. 'What do you want me to do?'

'I'm going to climb the tree and grab the life jackets. Why don't you tie our shirts together and follow me. If by chance I fall in, we can use the shirts as a rope, and I'll grab it.'

'It doesn't make a long rope,' said Jake, tying the sleeves of their work shirts together.

'It's better than nothing,' said Jody. 'Besides I'm not planning on having to use it.' Jody turned to start her climb up the tree. Then she stopped. She smiled at Jake, 'Thanks,' she said, softly.

Jake glanced up at his sister. 'Thanks for what?' he asked.

'For trusting me,' said Jody. 'Trusting my judgment and not arguing with me.'

Jake looked away. He and Jody rarely talked about their relationship. They had been in so many adventures together and through so much that they took each other for granted. Jake knew that Jody wasn't an easy person to get to know. She was courageous and smart, but she didn't like even her brother to know her moments of self-doubt, the moments when she was afraid.

'Good luck, Jody,' said Jake softly. Jake watched anxiously as Jody crept out over the river in her T-shirt and shorts. She clung to the branches of the cottonwood tree like a monkey. The smooth, swooping tongue of the main force of the river dashed back and forth at the rocks below her as if in obsessed fury that anything could stand in its way.

Inch by inch Jody crawled out on the tree until the life jackets were right below her. She glanced back at Jake who stood at the root of the tree. Jake raised his thumbs up. Then he crossed his fingers.

Jody stretched out along the trunk of the tree, wrapping her long legs around the scratchy bark. Then she reached down. Her fingers were a good five inches above the life jackets. She signalled Jake to come forward.

Jake inched his way out onto the tree. 'Get ready to throw the rope if I fall,' shouted Jody. The river was sending a constant spray of white water into her eyes. She struggled to keep her eyes open. She looked down at the life jackets, hanging on the branch a tantalizing few inches from her fingers. She knew she would have to loosen her grip on the tree trunk with her legs if she was going to be able to grab them. Slowly she unwrapped her legs and now was just balanced on the tree as if she were trying a complicated gymnastic trick on a particularly rough balance beam.

Jake hadn't realised he was holding his breath until he had to gasp for air. But Jody's hand had grasped the life jackets and she had pulled them up to her chest. Very carefully she inched her way back to Jake.

Even though the sun hadn't reached the river yet, Jody was drenched with sweat. Jake smiled at her and leaned back against the canyon wall.

'I think I just turned eighteen,' said Jake. 'I feel like I've aged four years.'

Jody looked at Jake's curly red hair critically. 'Come to think of it, I think I do see a few grey hairs. Did you know people actually can turn grey overnight? Your hormones react to the shock and take all the pigment out of your hair roots.'

'Yes, well – do you think we could have a moratorium on odd facts for a while?' asked Jake.

Jody grinned. She handed him one of the life jackets.

'Okay, now that we have them, now that you've risked your life for them, what good are they?' asked Jake. 'Without a boat, we're still stuck here.'

Jody didn't answer him right away. She looked downstream. They had walked past the worst part of the rapids. After a few more boulders, the river bed widened out again, giving the water a chance to rush by with less fury.

'We can get down the river in the life jackets,' said Jody. 'Just like Eric taught us to do.'

'You're nuts,' said Jake flatly.

Jody's eyes narrowed. 'You knew what I had in mind when I climbed out to get those life jackets,' she insisted. 'Why are you calling me nuts now?'

'Because now that we have the life jackets I realise how crazy it is. We can't go down the river in our life jackets.'

'We would if we had been in a raft and the raft tipped,'

85

insisted Jody. 'They're designed to keep our heads above water.'

'I wish *you* had been designed to keep your head out of hot water,' muttered Jake.

Jody ignored him. She started to strap on the life jacket.

Jake looked down at the river doubtfully. 'You really think we can survive bouncing down that river in a life jacket?' he asked.

'We've already walked past most of Big Drop,' said Jody. 'As I see it, we can ride that big tongue past those three big boulders, and then the water seems to calm down. We can rest by that next sandbar.'

'If we get there,' said Jake, but he took the life jacket from Jody.

'Come on,' said Jody. 'You were always the optimist in the family.'

'Yeah,' said Jake. 'That was before I turned grey.'

17

SUNK AND DOWN

Jake knew the canyon had walls, but he didn't see them. All he felt and saw was the tremendous force of the river as it carried him bobbing downstream. Miraculously the life jacket lifted his head and neck above the water. Jake discovered that because of the life jacket's construction he didn't have to struggle to keep the correct position. The life jacket more or less forced the correct position on him – legs bent in a sitting position.

Up ahead of him, he could see Jody's orange jacket bobbing in front of him. He didn't know how fast they were going. It felt like sixty miles an hour, but Jake knew that it couldn't be that fast.

Time seemed to have stopped completely. There only seemed to be distance. Later Jody and Jake would estimate that they had bobbed in the river no more than ninety seconds but each second had its own taste as Jake fought to keep the water out of his mouth and fought down the feeling of panic, trying to force himself to trust the construction of the life jacket.

Suddenly the river made a sharp turn and widened, immediately slowing its course. Just as suddenly Jody and

Jake both felt the other world exist again – the world of sky and cliffs and awareness of the colours – the red and grey of the cliffs, the silver of the limestone. For a quarter of a mile the river was calm.

Up ahead, Jake saw Jody struggle up onto a scrap of beach about twelve to fourteen feet wide. She waved to him, signalling him to try to come in.

'Easier said than done,' Jake muttered to himself as he tried to stop floating and actually swim to the shore. Luckily, the shoreline seemed to dip towards him, and Jake found that his feet could touch the bottom. He was grateful that Jody had insisted that they keep on their sneakers as his feet rolled around on the sharp rocks. Jake half crawled and half dragged himself up onto the beach. Jody ran to him.

'Are you all right?' she asked.

Jake nodded. He took off the life jacket and rolled on his back, trying to catch his breath. The sun felt wonderful, warming his body. The water had been cold.

Finally Jake sat up. When he did, he started coughing. 'I think I swallowed most of the Colorado River,' he sputtered.

'Me too,' said Jody. 'I had the feeling that water levels probably went down in California, I swallowed so much.'

'Don't make me laugh,' said Jake. 'It hurts.'

Now that they were momentarily out of danger, Jake realised how much his body had taken a beating from the power of the river.

'Well, at least we seem to have come out at the other end of Big Drop,' said Jody. She looked downstream. 'It's fairly calm here,' she said. 'Maybe it stays calm for a while. Let's walk downstream and see how far we can get and if we can see any more dangerous rapids.'

'Or dangerous people,' added Jake.

They walked along the narrow scrap of beach. The beach

followed the curve of the river. Suddenly Jake stopped short. 'Jody,' he whispered, 'look at this.'

Carved into a big black rock was an inscription.

CAMP NO. 7 HELL TO PAY
SUNK AND DOWN

'Do you think that's a code?' asked Jake.

Jody knelt beside the rock. The letters were worn and faint in part. Jody rubbed her fingers along the letters.

'It's no code,' said Jody. 'It's been here a long time. I remember reading about it. It was made in the last century. A boat crashed on a rock near here.'

'Terrific,' said Jake. 'Sunk and down. It sounds like it could be our motto.'

18

SATAN'S GUT

Jody led the way as they scrambled over the rocks. They were wearing their life jackets so they could have their hands free to balance themselves as they fought to find a footpath along the increasingly narrow shelf between the canyon and the river. The river had been practically brought to a standstill by the close-set rocks that lay like dangerous stepping stones from shore to shore.

'Do you see Satan's Gut?' shouted Jody. She pointed to the water below them. A strand of water gleamed in the sun, looking taut and glistening along the deepest part of the rapid. Looking down on it, it almost looked like the river had been laid open by some giant surgeon.

'We can't go down that in our life jackets!' shouted Jake above the noise of the river. 'I don't have the guts – to make a bad pun.'

'I don't have the guts either,' said Jody, looking at the raging water.

'I think you'd have to make a pact with the devil to get down that,' said Jake. 'That's where it must have got its name.'

'Wait a minute,' said Jody. 'I see something.' Jody scrambled down to the river's edge. Stuck in the flotsam of the eddy by the shore, she found an oar. She waved it to show Jake. Jake scrambled down to her side.

'It's from one of our boats,' said Jody excitedly. 'If they lost it, they can't be far. They must have had to camp nearby.' Jody examined the oar.

'What are you looking for?' asked Jake. 'A hidden message? More "Sunk and Down"?'

'Actually, I think the oar *is* a message,' said Jody. 'Just like the life preservers were a message. Someone is leaving us clues because they hope we're following them. We've got to go on.'

Jody threw the oar back down. 'Nothing is scratched on it. I thought maybe he'd have time to scratch a message. That message on the rock got my hopes up.'

Jody took the oar and shoved it into the river. Her eyes followed its path. It came to rest at the end of the rapids.

'Bull's-eye!' said Jody. 'If the oar survived without splintering, we can too. We've got to try. I'll go first, and if I get into trouble, you can fish me out.'

'Thanks a lot,' said Jake.

'You've got to admit that riding the river is a lot faster way of travelling than trying to scramble around the rocks,' argued Jody.

'Yeah,' said Jake. 'But we won't drown on the rocks.'

'Jake, we can't waste any more time,' urged Jody. 'If we don't reach them in time, Matt and his partner may decide they can travel easier without hostages. My guess is that someone is leaving us clues every time they go through white water. One of his prisoners *wants* us to follow, *needs* us. Whenever they go through a rapid, someone throws us out a clue. After all, you can't hold a gun steady on those rapids, but if one of his hostages wasn't worried, they wouldn't have thrown us these life preservers or thrown out the oar.'

'Okay, you convinced me,' said Jake. 'Let's go.'

'I'll go first,' said Jody. 'Remember to wait until you see whether I make it or not.'

'I wish you wouldn't put it that way,' said Jake seriously.

Jody nodded. Then she smiled. 'And only a few days ago, back home, you were worried about getting on a little, tiny plane.'

'Right,' said Jake. 'In fact, how do I know that you didn't engineer this whole thing just so you wouldn't have to get back on the plane? Remember, you were much more frightened of the airplane ride than I was.'

'Actually,' said Jody, 'after this trip, any airplane ride will seem like a piece of cake.'

She lowered herself into the river. Jake watched as she was swept downstream, the life jacket keeping her head above the waves. She grabbed hold of a tree trunk and pulled herself to shore and then waved to Jake to follow her.

'I hope we're not going to make a habit out of this,' Jake muttered to himself. He held on to a large granite rock and started to lower himself into the widest part of the wave. It curled in on itself, a pretty caramel colour from the silt, with a white pompadour. Just as he let go of the rock to slip into the wave Jake gasped in horror. He was staring down, down, down into a monstrously thrashing whirlpool just three feet from his left hand. Desperately he tried to swim to the right to avoid the hole.

He glanced back over his shoulder. He saw the foam of the whirlpool swirling. He kicked with his legs as hard as he could. He felt himself hanging on the edge, and if he had thought time had stood still before, he realised he had known nothing of how long time could stop.

Later he would remember that his life did *not* flash before his eyes. Instead, his only thought was to escape. His mind and body had only one goal – to keep him out of the abyss.

He made one last violent scissor kick and then a last-chance current skirting the brim of the whirlpool caught Jake and sent him down Satan's Gut.

He landed at Jody's feet. Jody held out her hand and pulled him to shore. Jake's legs were trembling. He held on to his stomach.

'Jake, are you okay?' Jody demanded. Jake shook his head back and forth.

'No,' he managed to croak, and then he threw up all the silty water he had swallowed. When he finished he was still shaking. 'Are you trying to get us killed?' Jake demanded.

'What are you talking about?' asked Jody. 'What's wrong with you? This ride was a piece of cake compared to the last one we took.'

'Didn't you see that whirlpool?' Jake shrieked.

Jody stared at her brother. 'What whirlpool?' she asked, her voice betraying her fear.

'The whirlpool I almost went to the bottom of,' said Jake. Getting angry seemed to help him get over his fear. He paused. 'Did you really not see it at all?' he asked.

'I didn't even see it,' said Jody, her voice barely a whisper. 'If you had been caught in it, I wouldn't have been able to save you, and it would have been all my fault.'

Jake stopped trembling. Usually Jody was the brave one. Jake knew that Jody didn't mind risking her life, but she wouldn't be able to live with the thought that she was responsible for his risking his life.

'Hey, stop being a martyr,' said Jake. 'I'm here, and even if I had been caught in the whirlpool it wouldn't be your fault. Nobody pushed me when I went in. Nobody ever pushes me when I join you in our adventures. It's always my choice.'

Jody sighed. 'It's strange, isn't it, Jake?' she said thoughtfully. 'Out here in the wilderness we're saying things to each other that we never said before.'

'I guess we never felt we had to say them before,' said Jake seriously.

19

HUNGER PAINS

Jake looked up the canyon wall. The late afternoon sun was crawling up towards the rim. Jake shivered. 'I would give a lot for a sleeping bag tonight,' he said. 'One night alone in the cave was an adventure. Two nights is beginning to feel too much like a nightmare that's never over.'

Jody and Jake looked downstream at several small ripples. The rocks no longer crowded the river, and Jody and Jake could walk along the shoreline.

'In the morning we should be able to stay out of the water,' said Jody. She wasn't anxious to force Jake back into the dangerous current.

'Let's worry about the morning in the morning,' said Jake. 'Right now I'm worried about a dry place to sleep. Do you think we should walk a little bit before it's dark, or should we just try to make a fire here?'

Jody didn't answer Jake. She seemed absorbed in her own thoughts.

'Come on,' said Jake. 'Don't leave me out again. What are you thinking about?'

'I'm just trying to figure out which of the three of them is Matt's partner,' answered Jody. 'I can't think of anything else. Who do you think it is?'

'The mysterious partner,' said Jake. He sounded bitter. 'It seems like we're going around in circles, caught in a whirlpool. I guess Jesse is the most likely.'

'I don't know,' said Jody. 'I liked Jesse, even though he was a daredevil. Why should he have saved me from the scorpion? I hate to think it was Eric either.'

'Well, I liked Alison,' said Jake. 'If you want to make it a popularity contest, I sort of liked all of them. I even liked Matt – at least a little.'

'What about Alison?' suggested Jody. 'She's not exactly a pussycat when it comes to taking risks.'

'Neither is Jesse or Eric. Besides, I can't imagine Alison doing anything to hurt us,' argued Jake.

'If you ask me, there's more than a little sexism going on. You don't want to think of Alison as guilty just because she's a woman.'

'Hope Diamond,' said Jake unexpectedly.

Jody stared at him. 'Excuse me. Hope Diamond. Is that the punch line to a joke?'

'No,' said Jake thoughtfully. 'Alison Hope, Matt Diamond. You're right. I might have been blinded by the fact that Alison's a woman.'

'I get you,' said Jody, suddenly reading Jake's mind. 'If Matt and Alison are related, and Matt was picking a false name, his subconscious might make him pick something related to Hope – like Diamond.'

'Alison does like to play with words,' said Jake. 'Only somehow I still can't imagine her going along with any plan that meant just abandoning us.'

'All this is pretty academic anyhow,' said Jody. 'Until we find them, it doesn't matter.'

'And you call me the optimist,' muttered Jake.

'What does that mean?' demanded Jody.

'I just like the way you said *until*, as if there was no question that we were going to catch up with them in the wilderness.'

'Well, I never saw the sense of being a pessimist,' said Jody. 'If something bad happens, it's going to happen anyway. Why waste time worrying?'

'How about worrying about a safe and dry place to sleep tonight,' said Jake. 'In fact, if you want to be an optimist, how about a motel with room service. I sure wouldn't mind picking up a phone right now and ordering a cheeseburger.'

'Don't think about food,' warned Jody.

'Good advice to the starving,' said Jake.

Jody looked concerned. 'Are you starving?' she asked.

'Let me put it this way,' said Jake. 'The two sides of my stomach are meeting for the first time, and I don't think they like each other. From the grumblings and rumblings it feels like they're getting ready to fight World War Three in there.'

'That's graphic enough,' said Jody. She looked around at the scrub bushes growing near the river and the few cottonwood trees. 'I wish I knew which plants we could eat,' she said. 'I'm sure some of these are edible.'

Jake got down on all fours and examined the plants. Growing near the ground he found a small ground-hugging plant no more than two inches high. Small delicate yellow flowers clung to the tiny leaves.

'Purslane!' shouted Jake. 'They eat it in India. I should have remembered that it grows in dry climates.' Jake handed a bunch of weeds to his sister.

Jody bit into it. White ooze dripped from the stem. The weed tasted bitter. Jody spat it out. 'Yuk!'

'Yuk, nothing,' said Jake. 'It's got vitamin C and carbohydrates. Eat it.'

'You're right,' said Jody, taking another bite. 'Tomorrow we may get weak from hunger.' She took another bite and swallowed it. 'How come you know about this and I don't?' she asked.

'Because I always pay more attention to food,' answered Jake. He munched on the weed. 'People in India and Persia have been eating this for two thousand years.'

'I wouldn't mind if I didn't eat it again for two thousand years,' said Jody, struggling to get down another mouthful. Then she stopped, almost in mid-swallow, and cocked her head. 'Do you smell something?' she asked. 'Steak!'

Jake kept eating his bitter weed. 'You're hallucinating,' he said. 'You know, you want steak and all of a sudden you smell steak. I've read of things like this happening.'

Jody stood up and faced downstream. 'The wind is coming from the west,' she said. 'Jake, I'm not hallucinating. It's steak. Come on!'

'I'm eating the first meal we've had in twenty-four hours and you want me to go on a wild steak hunt. I don't smell anything.'

But Jody was already walking downstream. Reluctantly Jake got up and followed her. Then the wind shifted and Jake raised his nose in the air as if he were a hound dog picking up a scent.

The distinctive odour of charcoal-grilled steak hit his nostrils and seemed to travel right down to his stomach. It was as if his stomach physically tasted the steak.

He caught up to Jody in a hurry. 'Steak!' he whispered. 'You're right.'

'Shhh,' Jody warned. 'We've got to be careful.'

But all Jake could think about was eating.

20

AN OUTLAW'S OLD TRICK

As they followed their noses, Jake quickened the pace. Then he suddenly bent down and picked up something.

'Look,' he said to Jody. He showed her a piece of driftwood. It had been moulded by the river into the perfect replica of a gun.

'Are you planning on shooting off splinters?' asked Jody sarcastically.

'I just thought it might come in handy,' said Jake.

'I'm not going to let you get in a showdown with Matt. He has a real gun, remember.'

Jake swallowed hard. He was about to throw away his piece of driftwood, but it felt good in his hand and he kept it.

They continued another hundred yards. They heard voices before they saw the campsite. The canyon walls were very close to the river at this point, and Jody and Jake could barely pick a path along the shoreline. Up ahead the shoreline widened, and they could see a raft tied up to a lone cottonwood tree. A fire was glowing in the distance.

Jody put up a warning hand to Jake, urging him to keep quiet. She pointed up the cliff. Jake groaned silently to himself. Jake realised that even with his driftwood gun he and Jody couldn't burst into the campsite without first finding out what was going on.

They scrambled up the canyon wall. Luckily the roar of the river drowned out the noise of Jody and Jake climbing up the cliff to a point above the campsite. Looking down, they could see a campfire. The canyon's lip was just catching the last rays of the sun. Jody and Jake could make out four figures, but all four of them had their backs to the canyon wall, and Jody and Jake couldn't see any faces. Alison's auburn hair stood out. She was standing over the steaks by the campfire. Someone was standing next to her. Two others were sitting down near the one cottonwood tree. Jody and Jake couldn't tell whether those two were tied up or not.

Jake clutched his stomach. The smell of steak wafting up the canyon was almost more than he could bear. Jody whispered in his ear.

'We've got surprise on our side. I want to try something.'

'What?' whispered Jake anxiously. Suddenly his hunger pains disappeared.

'It's an old trick of Butch Cassidy and the Sundance Kid,' whispered Jody. 'We use the echoes of the canyon to our advantage.'

'Butch Cassidy and the Sundance Kid wound up dead,' said Jake.

'Not until they left this country for Bolivia,' said Jody. 'Trust me.'

'Where have I heard that before,' said Jake, sighing. He watched in agony as one of the figures below took a steak off the fire. Jody reached behind her and gathered several small rocks. She handed them to Jake and then gathered several for herself. Jake started to put down his little piece of driftwood. But somehow he felt it gave him luck, so he shifted it to his left hand.

Jody put her finger to her lips and then gestured for Jake to follow her. When they were close to the campsite, Jody flung her rock backward at the canyon wall. It bounced off and ricocheted to the other rocks, causing a *rat-tat-tat* noise almost like a bullet.

Matt Diamond jumped up fast. He threw his steak to the ground. Jake saw his face, but Matt twirled away from Jody and Jake toward the sound of Jody's rock. Jody nodded to Jake. He threw his rocks.

Matt shouted. He moved farther away from Jody and Jake towards the sound of the rock. Jody grabbed a branch of a dead cottonwood tree and darted forward. She swung the branch and caught Matt unawares, knocking his gun out of his hand and felling him to the ground.

Jake ran into the campsite behind Jody. He held up his piece of driftwood and waved it in the air. 'Don't move, anybody. We've got you covered,' he said.

Alison stood there, her mouth wide open. Matt stirred. Suddenly Alison leaped forward. 'Don't move!' warned Jake, holding up his piece of driftwood menacingly. Alison ignored him. She grabbed Matt Diamond's real gun and in one quick move hit Matt over the head with it. Then she sat, or rather fell, down into a heap. She flung the gun away from her into the dirt. Jody ran and picked it up.

The whole incident from the moment Jody had thrown the first rock until Alison knocked out Matt Diamond had taken less than a minute.

Jody stared at the gun in her hand.

'Jody! Jake!' shouted Eric.

'Untie us!' shouted Jesse.

Jody came out of her daze. She glanced at Alison, then ran to Eric and Jesse. Jody untied them. She wiped away a tear. She hadn't realised she was crying. Eric put his arms around her.

'Thank God, you're safe,' he said. 'Did you get help? Where are the police?'

'There are no police,' said Jody.

'But we heard the sound of gunshots. Where did you get a gun?' Eric was so excited that his voice almost cracked.

Jake showed him his piece of driftwood.

'You came after us with *that*?' shrieked Eric.

'Yes,' said Jake. 'We figured the situation was desperate.'

'It was,' admitted Eric. 'Matt was planning on using us as hostages. *He* is the escaped killer, you know. And he's Alison's brother. As soon as we got out of the wilderness, Matt was going to insist that the authorities meet him with a small plane. He was going to force me to fly him to Mexico. He told us he would let us go then. I didn't know whether to believe him or not. I felt there was a slim hope that you and Jody might be picked up by a ranger or another rafting party. I knew the chances were slim. I never in a million years would have thought you could have followed us without a raft.'

'When we found those life jackets we thought you meant for us to follow,' said Jody.

'Without a raft!' exclaimed Jesse. 'Even I'm not the kind of daredevil who'd go down those rapids in a life jacket.'

'We walked around the most dangerous parts,' explained Jody. She looked up at Eric. She was glad he and Jesse were safe. 'How did you manage to throw out the life jackets if Matt had a gun on you?'

'Whenever we were going down tough rapids, Matt couldn't keep his gun on us, and I think he sensed that Alison wasn't wholeheartedly on his side. Matt made us take off our life jackets so we wouldn't jump overboard and try to escape. I flung them on the tree just to give whoever was looking for us a clue that we were still on the river and Matt hadn't taken us out over the canyon wall. Jesse flung the oar overboard. It just never occurred to me that you'd follow us without help.'

'Or to Matt or Alison,' said Jody. 'The element of surprise was what saved us.'

At the sound of her name Alison looked up. She had been crying. Jody walked over to her. 'Matt Hope is his real name, isn't it?' Jody asked. She pointed to Matt's collapsed form.

Alison nodded. 'Matt worried about you from the beginning,' she said. 'He thought you were a natural snoop.'

'You must have been worried about me too,' said Jody. 'You stole my newspaper.'

'I did,' said Alison. 'I was a wreck. Matt called me the day before we were supposed to go on the trip. He had escaped. He needed my help. You have to understand, he's my brother – just like you and Jake.'

'But he's a convicted killer,' exclaimed Jake. 'Even if he's your brother . . . I . . .'

'But I always thought he was innocent,' protested Alison. 'Matt was convicted of killing someone in a holdup. He held up a liquor store with three of his friends. Somehow the owner pulled out a gun, and one of the kids shot the owner in a panic. The other kids said that it was Matt, but Matt said he didn't do it. He claimed the other three ganged up on him. The jury didn't believe him and convicted him. He got a mandatory twenty-five-year prison term. I believed him when he said he was innocent.'

Alison took a breath. It was as if once she had started talking she couldn't stop. 'Matt called me when he broke out. He has always depended on me. His jail break wasn't planned. One of the guards happened to take a break at the wrong moment. Matt was working in the kitchen and assigned to unloading supplies. He saw his chance to hide in the caterer's truck. Matt didn't know where he would go or how he would live.'

'Speaking of him,' said Jesse, 'don't you think we should tie him up before he comes to.'

'Good idea,' said Eric. He and Jesse bound Matt's hands and feet tightly.

'What about me?' asked Alison. 'I think you'd better tie me up too, so you can turn me in to the police.'

Jody looked at her compassionately. 'He's your brother,' she said softly.

'I didn't know what to do when I got his phone call,' said Alison. 'I couldn't make him go back to prison. We both grew up on the Colorado. I gave him my canoe. Then I flew back up to Salt Lake City so no one would suspect that I had helped him. I hoped Matt would get downstream and be safe. He planned on working his way to Mexico and he said he would try to straighten himself out down there. Instead, he wrecked the canoe. When we found him, I almost died. First he told you that stupid story that he was a sheriff. Then he put the scorpion in Jody's shoe. I knew then that he would do anything.'

'He doesn't seem like the kind of person who ever knows what he's doing,' said Jake. 'He seems to just make up plans out of thin air.'

'Why did he put the scorpion in my shoe?' asked Jody. 'Just out of meanness?'

'Maybe,' said Alison, her voice barely a whisper. 'He thought you suspected him — especially after I told him you had the newspaper with his picture in it.'

'I never got to see his picture,' said Jody. 'In fact, I suspected Jesse stole my newspaper.'

'Thanks,' said Jesse sarcastically. 'All I wanted was the comics.'

'Jake and I had time to suspect everybody,' admitted Jody.

'Well, Matt was most suspicious of *you*,' said Alison. 'I told him I had stolen your newspaper, and I didn't think you recognised him, but he wanted to get rid of you. He put the scorpion in your shoe without telling me.'

'A nice guy,' muttered Jake. 'How did he catch the scorpion in the first place?'

'With a cup,' said Alison. 'Matt always was quick with his hands. He let the scorpion loose in Jody's shoe, hoping she would get bitten. He thought if you got sick, he and I would take one of the rafts and leave you there. He wanted us to pretend we were going for help. I told him that I wouldn't have left you if you were in danger. We argued. That's when I began to get scared that Matt might do anything.'

'Whose idea was it to abandon us?' asked Jody. 'You would think if Matt had decided on hostages, he would want all of us.'

'I was the one who talked him into abandoning you,' admitted Alison. 'I was frantic after he tried that trick with the scorpion. I realised that he might have really killed that man in the liquor store. I didn't know what to do. I figured that you and Jake were the youngest – I'd try to get you out of danger first. I told Matt to leave you and that we should take Jesse and Eric as hostages. I told him it would be too awkward to have four hostages. I knew he had a gun in his backpack. He bought it with some money I gave him right after he escaped prison.'

'I was so shocked when he pulled the gun on us,' said Eric. 'I couldn't believe it.'

'He was my brother,' sobbed Alison. 'I had to help him. Matt was always getting in trouble. He started stealing things when he was in the third grade. Now I guess I'll have to go to jail, too, for helping him. I even helped him kidnap Jesse and Eric.'

'I don't know what I would have done if it had been Jake who was in trouble,' admitted Jody.

'Besides,' said Jake. 'At the last minute you were the one who conked him over the head.'

'I couldn't take it anymore,' said Alison. 'When you and Jody showed up out of the blue, I just wanted the whole thing to be over.'

'When we get back to civilisation, we can let the police straighten it out,' said Jody. 'If it turns out you need a lawyer, I bet we can talk Mom into helping.'

Jesse walked over to Jody. He put his arm around her shoulders. 'You're really something,' he said. 'I can't believe the risks you took coming down those rapids in a life jacket.'

'We didn't do it for the thrill,' said Jody. 'We did it because we knew your lives were in danger.'

'I know,' said Jesse. He kissed Jody lightly on the lips. 'I want to thank you for it.'

Jody blushed.

'Excuse me,' said Jake. 'All this talk is very enlightening, but do you think we could stop talking and eat. We haven't eaten since breakfast yesterday. It feels like it's been much longer.'

'Jake's right,' said Jody. 'The smell of those steaks is killing me.'

'Let's not have any talk about killing,' said Jake. 'Let's just eat.'

If you've enjoyed this book, you may
like to read some more Knight titles
in the same series

Post·A·Book

Elizabeth Levy

The Case of the Frightened Rock Star

Jody Markson is organising a rock concert to raise money to rebuild the school sports stadium, starring Michael Harper, a famous teenage rock musician and former student of the High School.

But a series of practical jokes, from red paint spilt over a batch of newly-printed posters to a mugging at the stadium, threatens to spoil all Jody's plans. It's as though someone wants to discourage her – in a most sinister and menacing way.

Another puzzle is Michael Harper himself – tense, nervous and frightened. 'It's as if I stumbled into quicksand,' said Jody. 'Everything about this concert seems treacherous, and I don't understand it.'

What can be behind it all? With only a few days to the concert, Jody and her brother Jake are determined to find out – and to expose the mysterious invisible joker.

The first Jody and Jake Mystery

Knight Books

Elizabeth Levy

The Case of the Counterfeit Racehorse

Jody and Jake are spending their summer holidays working at the stables attached to a nearby racecourse.

Jody loves horses, and she has a special way with a nervous and unhealthy racehorse named Pure Energy. But she is taken aback when after a short stay at the vet's, Pure Energy seems to make an astonishing recovery without her help.

Meanwhile, Jody experiences a succession of unfortunate 'accidents'. Mr Barrett, the stable owner, decides she is a liability and fires her. Torn between anger and disappointment, Jody is not sure what she misses more – the stables or Mr Barrett's son Peter.

Then when Pure Energy wins a surprising victory, and Mr Barrett is accused of fixing the race, Jody begins to suspect there's more to Pure Energy's performance than meets the eye.

The second Jody and Jake Mystery

Knight Books

Elizabeth Levy

The Case of the Fire-Raising Gang

Cycling home from school one day, Jody and Jake witness a fire in the run-down district of Northtown. Arson is immediately suspected and Mark Brown, a teenage gang leader and a pupil at Jody's school, is accused of the crime.

But despite the evidence – Mark's fingerprints on an empty paraffin can and a previous charge of arson – Jody is convinced Mark is being framed.

But how can she prove it? Mark's gang, the Bullets, is too suspicious to be helpful and though Jody soon has a list of suspects drawn from the Bullets and the rival Razor gang, she is not happy: 'I keep feeling that there is something we have definitely missed . . . some motive that we haven't even thought of yet.'

Then when someone sets fire to Jody's bicycle – a kind of sinister warning against asking questions – Jody stumbles on the vital clue. The stakes are higher than she had at first thought possible . . .

The third Jody and Jake Mystery

Knight Books

Elizabeth Levy

The Case of the Mile High Race

Jody Markson is not into athletics – unlike her father and brother – but when she becomes a target for a mystery gun-man or woman she surprises herself by the speed of her reactions.

She and her brother Jake are staying in Aspen, a glamorous mountain holiday resort, while their father attends a conference there which is attempting to reach a compromise on the problems of financing amateurs in sport.

The week's climax is a ten kilometre run, with enormous cash prizes for the winners or their clubs, and the atmosphere is tense as the world-class runners prepare.

But the shooting is only the first of many frightening events that week, and Jody and Jake must find out who is behind these vicious attacks before it's too late.

The fifth Jody and Jake Mystery

Knight Books

More mysteries from Knight Books

All these books are available at your local bookshop or newsagent, or can be ordered direct from the publisher. Just tick the titles you want and fill in the form below.

Prices and availability subject to change without notice.

KNIGHT BOOKS, P.O. Box 11, Falmouth, Cornwall.

Please send cheque or postal order, and allow the following for postage and packing:

U.K. – 45p for one book, plus 20p for the second book, and 14p for each additional book ordered up to a £1.63 maximum.

B.F.P.O. and EIRE – 45p for the first book, plus 20p for the second book, and 14p per copy for the next 7 books, 8p per book thereafter.

OTHER OVERSEAS CUSTOMERS – 75p for the first book, plus 21p per copy for each additional book.

Name ....

Address ....

....